Musical Beginnings: for Teachers and Students

Corrections
P. 110
P. 112

Time Value - Duration of musical notes

Rhythm - Progression of beats through time

Pitch - The highness or lowness of a tone.

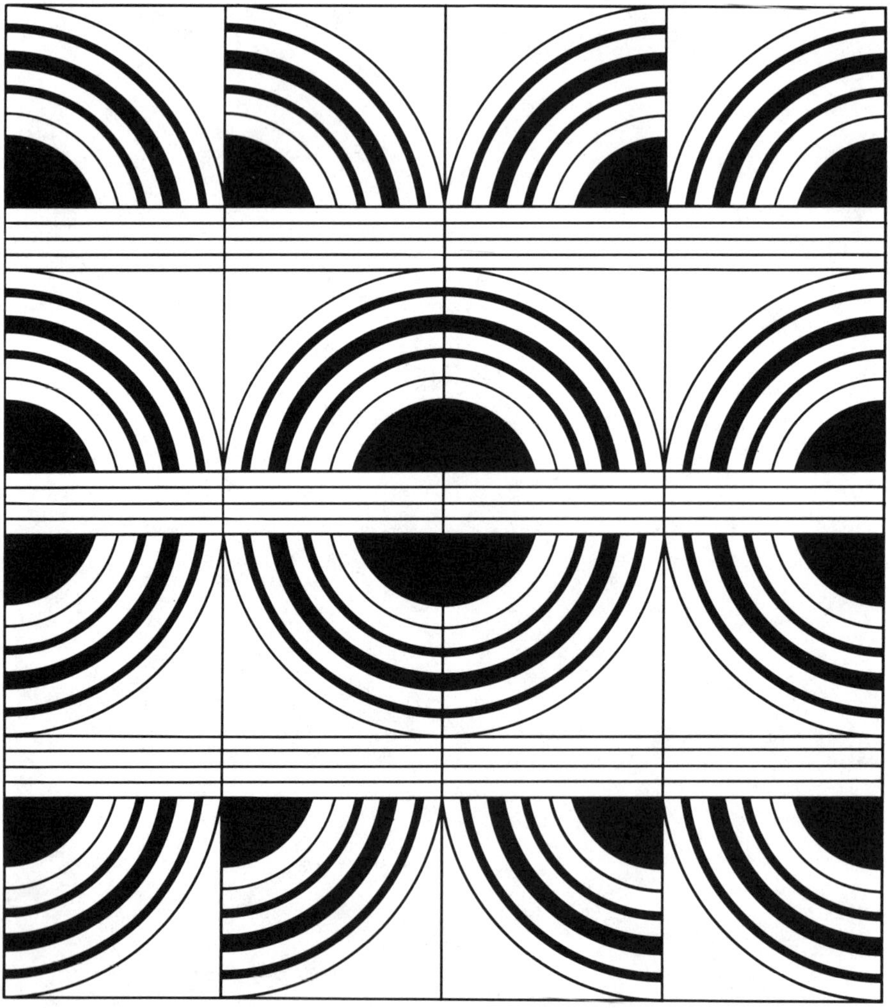

Musical Beginnings: for Teachers and Students

Gary M. Martin

University of Oregon

Wadsworth Publishing Company, Inc.
Belmont, California

*To my mother,
whose steadfast commitment to music
ensured my musical education*

Designer: Ann Wilkinson
Music Editor: Edward Eldredge
Production Editor: Suzanne Knott

© 1975 by Wadsworth Publishing Company, Inc.
Belmont, California 94002

All rights reserved. No part of this book may be reproduced, stored in a retrieval system or transcribed, in any form or by any means, electronic, mechanical, photocopying, recording or otherwise, without the prior written permission of the publisher.

ISBN: 0-534-00385-2

L. C. Cat. Card No.: 75-3956

Printed in the United States of America

3 4 5 6 7 8 9 10/79 78

Preface

Although most students have had some exposure to music, many arrive in introductory courses with an inadequate understanding of its fundamental principles. Moreover, their widely varied musical backgrounds have produced individual "gaps" that seldom coincide.

Musical Beginnings is designed to provide the *specific* knowledge each student lacks in order to bring the class to a uniform level of understanding from which the teacher may proceed. The book format was carefully tested and revised to perform this function. A "branching" program tests the students' understanding of each concept before it is explained. Thus, students who can answer the *Diagnostic Question* for a particular concept move quickly to the next one. If they cannot answer the question, they receive either a short review of the subject or a lengthy explanation--according to their self-determined need. Students spend time only on the concepts they don't understand, working always at their own speed and at their own levels of understanding.

Six features the author has found lacking in most elementary music books have been incorporated into this text:

1. *A careful presentation of music fundamentals.* Study is organized in units that cover the basic components of music notation, rhythm, melody, harmony, intervals and chords, major and minor tonalities, and structure (i.e., phrase, motive, period, and binary and ternary forms).

2. *An exciting approach to programmed instruction.* Concepts are presented in small steps as in linear programs, but there are several alternate routes through the material, each with a unique mode of presentation. The diverse techniques used in explanations and tests are intended to avoid the "pall" effect, which is inflicted on students and teachers alike by endless statements of fact in unvarying presentational styles.

3. *Proficiency developers.* Knowledge unlocks doors and gives us new capabilities, but only when we apply the knowledge to our experiences are these capabilities fully realized. For this reason, every chapter concludes with special activities that allow the student to bring the concepts into action.

4. *Self-tests*. Placed at the end of each chapter, these tests reinforce the students' knowledge, reveal the areas that still need review, and thus, teach as well as evaluate.

5. *Review indexes*. Combined with the self-test answers at the end of each chapter, the index directs students immediately to the part where they can review the test questions just missed.

6. *Chapters on elementary school music and teaching strategies*. The former explores vital musical experiences and specific objectives that clearly deserve attention at the elementary grade level. The latter concentrates on the teacher's classroom role and student-oriented learning strategies.

Undergraduate college students who tested and reviewed this book expressed enthusiastic approval with such comments as:

> These chapters served as a very good review, as I found that I had forgotten a lot. . . .

> . . .an interesting way for such a large class to become equated in musical knowledge in a fairly short time. . . .

> . . .more a game than a chore. . . .

> The chapters have been interesting, and I like moving at my own pace.

Music, of course, is an art that must be heard to be appreciated; the individual who desires to broaden his or her musical understanding must become involved with sound. Perhaps the best any book can do to further musical understanding is to imbue greater meaning to the creation and perception of musical sounds. Correct use of *Musical Beginnings* will certainly leave more time for actual involvement with music.

Gary M. Martin

Contents

Introduction   1

1
Basic Components of Music Notation   4

Staff and Great Staff
Treble Clef and Bass Clef Signs
Bar Lines and Measures
Time Values of Notes
Time Values of Rests
Range of Notes
Performance Markings and Dynamic Markings

2
Notational Components of Rhythm   51

Rhythm Identified
Mathematical Relationships of Musical Notes
Tied Notes, Dotted Notes
Meter Signatures and How They Determine Measure Content
Pickup Notes
Accent, Staccato, Tenuto, and Slur Markings

3
Notational Components of Melody   113

Definition of Pitch
Names of Notes in Treble Clef
Names of Notes in Bass Clef
Sharps, Flats, Naturals, and Ledger Lines
Octaves
Names of Notes on Piano Keyboard
Half Steps and Whole Steps
Concept of a Major Scale
Selected Key Signatures

4
Harmonic Structure of Music
207

Definitions of Harmony, Chord, and Interval
Identity of Basic Intervals
Concept of Major and Minor Intervals
Concept of Perfect, Augmented, and Diminished Intervals
Construction of a Triad
Major and Minor Triads
Inversions of Intervals and Chords
The I, IV, and V Chords

5
Major Scales, Chords, and Keys
257

Definitions of Key, Key Tone, Tonality, Scale, and Cadence
Position of Half Steps in Major Scales
Characteristics of Notes in Major Scales
Tonic SOL-FA System
Circle of Fifths for Major Keys
Major Key Signatures
Chord Names
Characteristics of Major Chords
Common Cadential Patterns

6
Minor Scales, Chords, and Keys
302

Differences Between Major and Minor Scales, Chords, and Keys
Two Different Kinds of Minor Scales
Circle of Fifths for Minor Keys
Relative Major and Minor Keys
Characteristics of Minor Chords
The i, iv, and V Chords in Minor Keys

7
The Structure of Music
334

Definitions of Phrase, Motive, Sequence, and Period
Phrases, Motives, and Periods in Musical Context
Definitions of Binary (Two-Part) and Ternary (Three-Part) Song Forms, Free Form, and Examples of Their Use in Musical Context
Relationship Between Cadences and Phrases

8
A Comprehensive View of School Music Programs   370

Three Primary Musical Behaviors
Three Domains of All Learning
Objectives of an Elementary Music Program
Elements of Music: Pitch, Rhythm, Timbre, Dynamics

9
Becoming the Right Kind of Teacher   395

The Nature of Learning
Motivation
Teacher-Oriented Presentational Strategy
Student-Oriented Activity Strategy
How to Evaluate Classroom Singing
RULEG System

Appendix   415

Major Key Signatures, Scales, and Chords
Minor Key Signatures, Scales, and Chords

Song Index   418

Index   419

Introduction

1

Programmed learning may be a new experience for you. This book is called a "scrambled" or "branching" program because the book cannot be read by turning consecutive pages. The book is divided into *parts*, each part a small, numbered unit of instruction. (You will frequently find two or three such numbers on one page.) Depending on your mastery of certain principles, you may skip parts devoted to their explanations. For example, from part 26 you may be instructed to turn to part 21 to continue reading. Therefore, when you finish reading each part, it is important to note where you read next.

At the end of each chapter are two features that will be of great value to you in your study. The first, *Proficiency Developers*, will help you translate musical concepts into useable skills. The second, *Self-Tests*, will help you discover the chapter topics you have mastered and the ones you need to review.

You have reached the end of part 1. Please turn to part 3.

2

Oops!!

You did not follow instructions but fell into the habit of reading pages in consecutive order. You cannot do this in a programmed textbook. Please return to part 1 and follow the directions.

3

Good. You have followed the first instruction encountered in your study.

On certain pages, you will see the caption *Use the Shield*. When so directed, you should use the shield (attached inside the front cover of the book) to conceal the page below the part you are reading. Complete instructions for its use are printed on the shield.

At frequent intervals in the book, *Diagnostic Questions* will test your knowledge of some musical concept. To the right of each alternative will be a part number. Select the answer you think is right and turn to the part indicated. There you will find whether or not your answer was correct. If it was correct, a new Diagnostic Question will be presented. If your answer was incorrect, an explanation will follow. If you are unsure of the answer or realize your answer would be a guess, choose the alternative "I'm unsure" (or one similarly worded). You will then be directed to a detailed discussion of the subject. Remember, your basic purpose in reading this book is to gain an understanding of the fundamentals of music. Honesty about what you know and don't know is imperative, and guessing will only impede your progress.

When you miss a question, you may be asked to reread certain parts. Be sure to read them even more carefully the second time, for you will probably meet the question again to test your adjustment since the initial mistake.

Because musical concepts build on each other, a secure knowledge of each topic is essential to understanding the next. Therefore, at the end of each chapter a *Self Evaluation Test* will help you to determine the amount you have learned--and whether or not you are ready to go on to the next chapter. You will have a chance to review any material that may still confuse you.

It is hoped that this book will be an interesting and informative experience for you. Go to part 4.

1
Basic Components of Music Notation

4

A musical sound is a fleeting experience. <u>To retain musical sounds for future reproduction, a system of notation was developed</u>, just as a system of writing was developed to record the spoken word. This chapter deals with the basic symbols and words that constitute the modern music notational system. Chapter 1 contains seven Diagnostic Questions.

Objectives

After completing this chapter, you should be able to identify correctly the following musical terms and their equivalent symbols.

1. A music staff, the great staff, and ledger lines.
2. The treble clef and bass clef signs.
3. A bar line and a measure.
4. Whole, half, quarter, and eighth notes.
5. Whole, half, quarter, and eighth rests.
6. The highest and lowest notes in a musical passage.

You should also be able to identify the action specified by each of the following words or symbols that are used in musical notation.

1. Crescendo ⟨
2. Decrescendo ⟩
3. D.C. (da capo)
4. D.S. (dal segno)
5. Fine
6. Repeat sign: ‖: :‖

Now go to part 5.

Diagnostic Question One

In the example below are some musical symbols, numbered 1-6. Choose the alternative that correctly matches the numbered symbol with its name.

Then turn to the part indicated. There you will learn whether your answer is correct. If you are not sure of the names of the symbols, choose alternative a. Remember—no guessing.

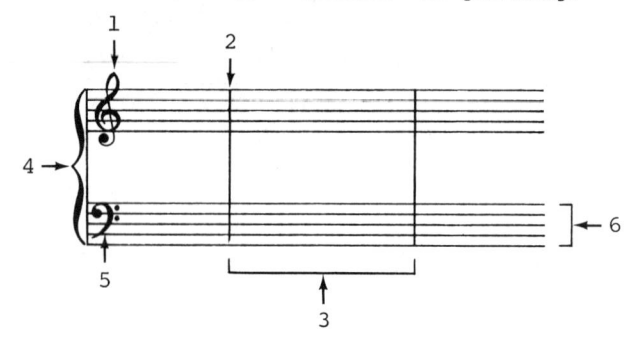

Alternatives

			part
a.	I am unsure. Please explain this.		6
(b.)	1 - treble clef sign 2 - bar line 3 - measure	4 - great staff 5 - bass clef sign 6 - staff lines	13
c.	1 - bass clef sign 2 - bar line 3 - measure	4 - great staff 5 - treble clef sign 6 - staff lines	19
d.	1 - treble clef sign 2 - measure 3 - bar line	4 - staff lines 5 - bass clef sign 6 - great staff	15

You have helped yourself by stating frankly that you are not familiar with all or some of these six musical symbols, and the following discussion will help you identify them.

Five lines placed together, as shown on the right, form a STAFF.

When two staves are used together they are called the GREAT STAFF.

On the great staff, special signs are used to designate the top staff, called the TREBLE CLEF, and bottom staff, called the BASS CLEF. The sign for the top staff looks like this: 𝄞 . It is called the TREBLE CLEF SIGN.

Perhaps you know that a male singer with a very low voice is called a BASS. The sign for the bottom staff, the BASS CLEF SIGN, looks like this: 𝄢 .

Complete the following statements.

Use the Shield

When we use these signs in music notation we have a _____ staff with treble clef and bass clef signs.

☙

great

The sign for the bottom staff is the _____ clef sign.

☙

bass

The _____ clef sign identifies the top staff.

☙

treble

Go to part 7.

7

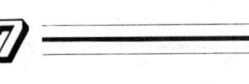

Use the Shield

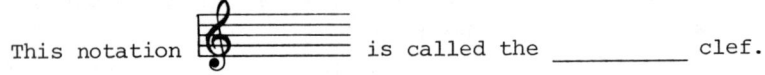

This notation 𝄞 is called the _____ clef.

☙

treble

The treble clef is the top staff, and the bottom staff is the _____ clef.

☙

bass

When the treble cleff and the bass clef are joined together like this, we have an example of the _____ .

☙

great staff

Put the Shield Aside

The staff can be divided into sections with vertical lines called BAR LINES. The distance between any two bar lines is called a MEASURE.

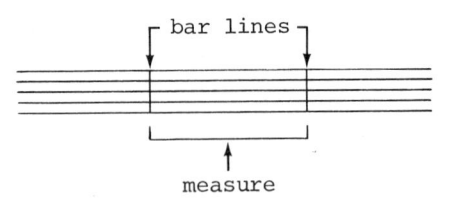

In the example below, there are three bar lines and two measures.

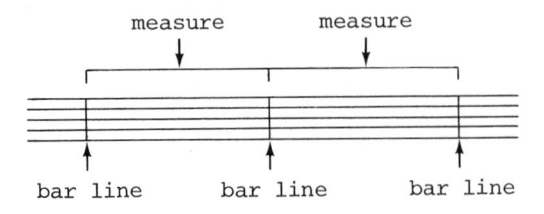

Turn to part 8.

8

Use the Shield

This distance ⊟ is called a _____ .

~

measure

A measure is the distance between two _____ _____ .

~

bar lines

Put the Shield Aside

Fill in the blank spaces below to correctly identify each of the notational symbols shown. Then check your answers with the key in part 12.

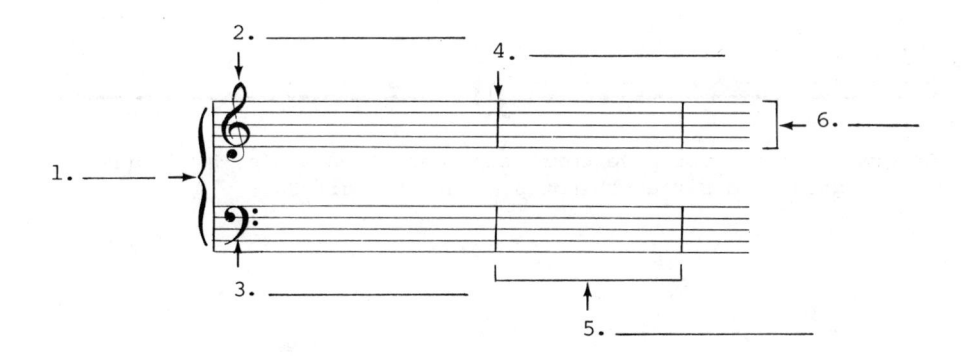

9

That example tripped you up. To find out why, turn to part 14.

=========== 10 ===========

The alternative you selected contained an error.

Let's look at those notes again:

𝅝 - whole note

𝅗𝅥 - Add a stem and you get a half note.

♩ - Fill in the note and it becomes a quarter note.

♪ - Put a flag on it and it is an eighth note.

𝅘𝅥𝅯 - Put two flags on it and it is called a sixteenth note.

If you were to add still another flag, what would you have then? Of course, you would have a thirty-second note. (They are actually rather scarce.)

For further instruction, turn to part 21. If you are ready to answer the Diagnostic Question, turn to part 16.

=========== 11 ===========

Congratulations, you have correctly identified whole, half, quarter, eighth, and sixteenth notes. Turn to part 24.

12

Notational Symbols:

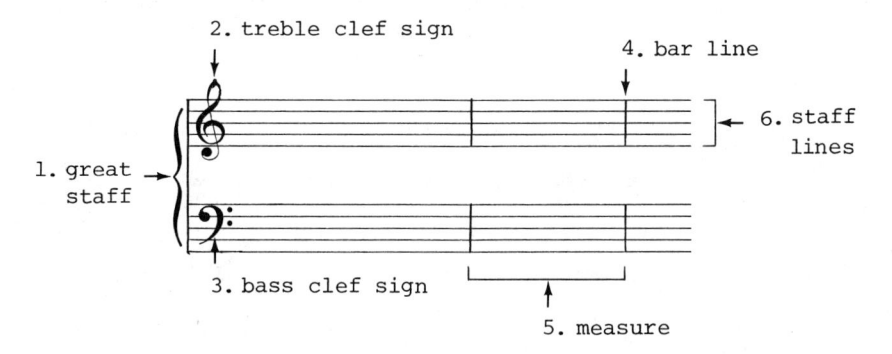

1. great staff
2. treble clef sign
3. bass clef sign
4. bar line
5. measure
6. staff lines

Now return to part 5 and answer the Diagnostic Question.

13

Right! The names of the musical symbols are given below. I'm glad you have identified them.

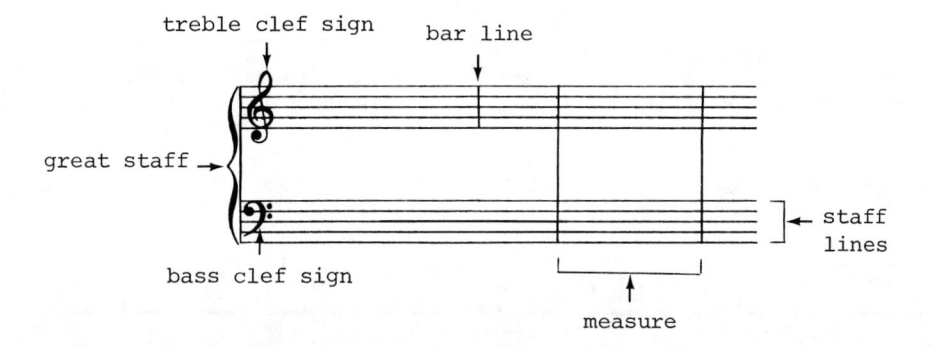

- treble clef sign
- bar line
- great staff
- bass clef sign
- measure
- staff lines

Having demonstrated that you know the basic framework for music notation, you are ready to consider the notation of musical rhythm.

Go to part 16.

14

It will take only a short time to learn these note values. In music, the notes are assigned the mathematical values of whole (1/1), half (1/2), quarter (1/4), eighth (1/8), and sixteenth (1/16). The symbols for these notes are simply and logically constructed.

1. An elliptical circle is a WHOLE note: 𝆓
2. Put a stem on the whole note and it becomes a HALF note: ♩
3. Fill in the half note and it becomes a QUARTER note: ♩
4. Put a flag on the stem of the quarter note and it becomes an EIGHTH note: ♪
5. Put a second flag on the stem of the eighth note and it becomes a SIXTEENTH note: ♬

We now have the following symbols:

𝆓 = whole note
♩ = half note
♩ = quarter note
♪ = eighth note
♬ = sixteenth note

The duration of the whole note (𝆓) is four times as long as the duration of the quarter note (♩). The time value of the whole note is therefore four times as great as the time value of the quarter note.

Now turn to part 21.

15

There seems to be something about this example that confuses you. By selecting this alternative, you indicated that you must have known something about music, or you would have chosen the alternative "I'm unsure." For an explanation of the six basic symbols, turn to part 19.

16

Diagnostic Question Two

To refer to the relative duration of musical notes we will use the term TIME VALUE. A note's time value indicates how long it is held in relation to other notes. The most common time values are represented by the whole note, half note, quarter note, eighth note, and sixteenth note, which are shown below. You must identify them. Again, there are four alternative responses. After choosing your alternative, turn to the appropriate part.

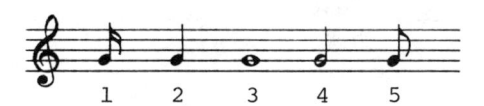

Alternatives

			part
a.	I'm not familiar with these time values.		14
b.	1 - eighth note 2 - quarter note 3 - whole note	4 - half note 5 - sixteenth note	10
c.	1 - sixteenth note 2 - eighth note 3 - whole note	4 - half note 5 - quarter note	9
(d.)	1 - sixteenth note 2 - quarter note 3 - whole note	4 - half note 5 - eighth note	11

17

Instead of an unequal pair, you chose a matched pair: the quarter note (♩) and quarter rest (𝄽). For an explanation go to part 28.

18

Complete the following exercise by filling in the blanks:

Use the Shield

This ▬ is a _____ rest.

🙰

half

This 𝄾 is a(n) _____ rest.

🙰

eighth

This 𝄽 is a _____ rest.

🙰

quarter

The whole rest is written (*above/below*) the line.

🙰

below

This ▬ is a _____ rest.

🙰

whole

The two rests 𝄽 and 𝄾 are _____ and _____ rests.

🙰

quarter, eighth

Of the rests 𝄽 , 𝄾 , and 𝄾 , which has the greatest time value?

🙰

quarter rest

Go to part 31.

19

You identified some of the symbols correctly, but others incorrectly.

Five horizontal lines placed together are called the STAFF or STAFF LINES.

When two staves are placed together, they are called the GREAT STAFF.

Special symbols are used on the great staff to differentiate the top staff, or TREBLE CLEF, from the bottom staff, or BASS CLEF.

The great staff is divided into sections by BAR LINES. The distance between two bar lines is called a MEASURE.

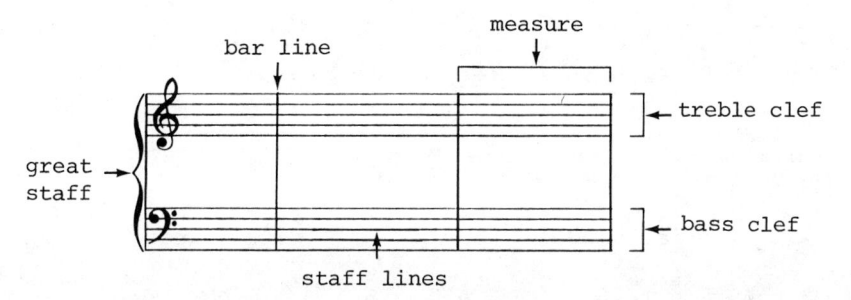

Return to the Diagnostic Question in part 5 and see if you can now answer it correctly.

20

You were asked to choose a pair unequal in time value, but you chose the eighth note (♪) and eighth rest (𝄾), which are correctly matched. For a review of this question, turn to part 28.

21

Answer the following questions:

Use the Shield

This (𝐨) is called a _____ note.

༄

whole

The whole note has the (*longest/ shortest*) time value of the notes on the right.

𝐨 𝅗𝅥 ♩ ♪ ♬

༄

longest

The note with the shortest time value in the above example would be the _____ note.

༄

sixteenth

This note (♩) is a _____ note.

༄

quarter

How many quarter notes does it take to equal one half note?

༄

two

Put the Shield Aside

Write the words whole, half, quarter, eighth under the appropriate notes. If you need a review, see part 14.

𝅗𝅥   ♪   ♩   𝐨

_____   _____   _____   _____

Now return to part 16 and see if you can answer the Diagnostic Question correctly.

22

Just follow this one very simple rule: THE HIGHER THE NOTE IS ON THE STAFF, THE HIGHER IT IS IN SOUND; THE LOWER THE NOTE IS ON THE STAFF, THE LOWER IT IS IN SOUND.

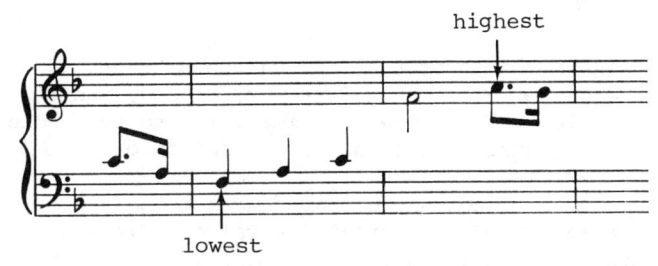

On the great staff, the pitch of the bass clef is lower than the pitch of the treble clef. When music becomes too low to be written conveniently on the treble staff, it is written on the bass staff. The illustration above is a good example of a melody using both staves.

Notes are written on staff lines and in the spaces between the lines. Notes very close to each other in pitch may appear on adjacent lines and spaces, a fact that demands careful observation by the inexperienced reader. Several examples of such adjacent notes are shown below.

Now carefully find the highest and lowest notes in the Diagnostic Question in part 34.

23

Not quite. It is easy to become confused about foreign words, as you just have. For an explanation that will help you remember them, read part 36.

24

Diagnostic Question Three

There are times in music when a brief silence, or a REST, is desirable. The symbols for the time values of rests are comparable to notes; there are whole, half, quarter, eighth, and sixteenth rests. The whole rest is equal in time value to the whole note; the half rest is equal to the half note, and so on.

In the example below, notes are paired with rests. All pairs except one contain symbols of equal time value. Find the UNEQUAL pair and turn to the designated part. (If you need a review of note values, turn to part 21.)

Alternatives

		part
a.	I'm not sure I know the symbols for rests. Please explain them to me.	28
b.	♩ = 𝄽	17
c.	♪ = 𝄾	20
(d.)	𝅗𝅥 = ▬	29
e.	𝅝 = ▬	33

25

That alternative is wrong. If you guessed at this answer, you did yourself an injustice. Only honest mistakes are understandable. Unless you actually learn the material, it is of no value to go through the motion of reading it. Please read on in part 22.

26

Good. You are now ready to learn the meanings of musical directions that appear at the edge of the staff.

Diagnostic Question Five

Match the musical directions in column 1 with their proper descriptions in column 2.

A 1. D.S. (DAL SEGNO)   A. go to the sign
D 2. D.C. (DA CAPO)   B. the end
B 3. FINE   C. repeat sign
C 4. ‖: :‖   D. go to the beginning

Alternatives

		part
a.	I'm not sure. Please explain.	36
b.	1 = A 3 = C 2 = D 4 = B	35
c.	1 = D 3 = B 2 = A 4 = C	23
(d.)	1 = A 3 = B 2 = D 4 = C	32

27

Very good! Hang on now, you have almost finished the chapter. Turn to part 40.

28

Once you know the time values of notes, the time values of musical rests are easy to learn.

The WHOLE rest carries the largest time value, and the HALF rest the second largest. These two rests look very much alike, as you can see in the example below.

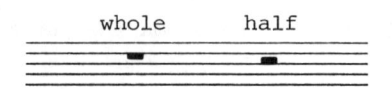

Here is a simple device to deep them from confusing you:

1. A whole rest (▀) is larger than a half rest in time value. Because it is larger (and therefore heavier), it hangs BELOW the staff line.
2. The half rest (▄) has a smaller time value than the whole rest. Because it is smaller (and therefore lighter), it sits ON TOP OF the staff line.

The next symbol (𝄽) is a quarter rest. Look at its shape carefully. The final symbols you need to recognize are the eighth and sixteenth rests. The eighth rest looks like this: 𝄾 . To make a sixteenth rest, just add another flag to the stem of the eighth rest: 𝄿 .

Can you guess how to make a thirty-second rest? Add another flag to the stem. Thirty-second rest: 𝅀 .

To review briefly:

▀ = whole rest (below the line)
▄ = half rest (above the line)
𝄽 = quarter rest
𝄾 = eighth rest
𝄿 = sixteenth rest

Go to part 18.

29

Right! Assuming yours was an honest answer—not just a good guess—you are now ready to consider pitch determination. For that, turn to part 34.

Put the Shield Aside

Let's add our words together now:

1. D.C. al fine means: go to the beginning and play to the word "fine."
2. D.S. al fine means: go to the sign 𝄋 and play to the word "fine."
3. Although it isn't Italian, you must also remember this symbol: ‖: :‖ (repeat sign). The arrows below show where to go when you see a repeat sign.

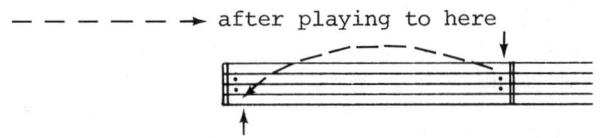

— — — — — → after playing to here

return to here and — — — — — — → play to the end.

Use the Shield

D.S. al fine means to go to _____ .

𝄋

the sign and play to the end.

This sign ‖: :‖ means that I should repeat the music that is found (*before/between/after*) the double bars.

𝄋

between

D.C. stands for which Italian words?

𝄋

Da Capo

BENE, ORA PARLA UN POCO ITALIANO (which means, "Good, now you speak a little Italian").

Now, return to part 26 and answer the Diagnostic Question.

31

Use the Shield

In the example on the right, only the _____ rest is correctly marked.

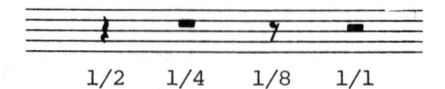

         1/2   1/4   1/8   1/1

☙
⅞ = 1/8

How many rests are correctly labeled?

         1/1   1/2   1/8   1/4

☙
two: ▬ = 1/1; ▬ = 1/2

If you made mistakes on this part or part 19, review the rest symbols again, beginning with part 28. If you made no mistakes, return to part 24 and answer the Diagnostic Question.

32

Molto bene! (That's Italian for "very good.") Now try another matching question, this time using dynamic markings, in part 37.

33

You were asked to choose a pair unequal in time value, but you chose an equal pair: the whole note (𝐨) and the whole rest (▬). Please go to part 28.

34

Diagnostic Question Four

Music is composed of notes that vary in pitch from low to high. Do you know how to distinguish the lower notes from the higher ones on the written page? From the example below, choose the alternative with the HIGHEST and the LOWEST notes, in that order.

Alternatives

				part
a.	I'm not sure.			22
	<u>high</u>	<u>low</u>		
b.	1 and	8		25
c.	1 and	5		38
(d.)	2 and	5		26

35

No, you have confused the repeat sign with the word FINE, which is the Italian counterpart of our word finish or END. Go to part 36.

If you understand the meanings of the Italian words, it will help you remember how they are used in musical context. D.S. are the initials for the Italian words DAL SEGNO (pronounced "doll SANE-yo"), which mean FROM THE SIGN. The sign referred to looks like this: 𝄋 . When you see D.S., you are supposed to GO BACK TO THE SIGN (𝄋) and begin playing from that point, thereby repeating the passage.

The second symbol was D.C., initials for the Italian words DA CAPO (pronounced "dah COP-oh"). "Capo" is similar to our English word "cap." The cap on a bottle is at the top. Da capo also means THE TOP. In music it means GO BACK TO THE TOP or GO BACK TO THE BEGINNING.

Now, for a review:

D.S. = go to the sign
D.C. = go to the beginning

The Italian word FINE (pronounced "FEE-nay") is related to the English word finish. It means simply STOP HERE`or THE END.

Fill in the blanks to complete these sentences:

Use the Shield

If I were playing a piece of music on the piano and I came to the initials D.S. I would go back to the _____ and play from there.

~
sign: 𝄋

If I came to the initials D.C. I would go back to the _____ .

~
beginning

The initials _____ _____ instruct me to return to this sign 𝄋 and play from there.

~
D.S.

Turn to part 30.

═══ 37 ═══

Diagnostic Question Six

Dynamic markings determine how loud or soft the music should be.
Dynamics in music are indicated by Italian abbreviations.

Below are two columns. Match the dynamic markings on the left with
the proper definition from the column on the right and select the
correct alternative.

       Markings   Definitions

E 1. pp (pianissimo)   A. loud
C 2. ff (fortissimo)   B. soft
B 3. p (piano)   C. very loud
A 4. f (forte)   D. medium soft
D 5. mp (mezzo piano)   E. very soft

Alternatives

                                                            part

a. I'm not sure. Where is the explanation?   39

b. 1 = E   4 = A
     2 = C   5 = B
     3 = D   42

(c.) 1 = E   4 = A
     2 = C   5 = D
     3 = B   27

d. 1 = C   4 = A
     2 = D   5 = E
     3 = B   41

═══ 38 ═══

No. You are right about the lowest note, but your choice of the
highest was wrong. Go to part 22.

All of the abbreviations p, pp, mp, f, ff, and mf refer to various degrees of loudness or softness of musical tone. If you can remember the meanings of just three letters, the dynamic markings will be easy to understand.

>p - SOFT   f - LOUD   m - MEDIUM

So, if you have two "f's" (ff), the symbol would mean doubly loud or better, VERY LOUD. Two "p's" (pp) would mean doubly soft or better, VERY SOFT. An "m" in front of either denotes moderation. Thus, "mp" means moderately soft, and "mf" means moderately loud.

Progressing from the softest sound on the left to the loudest sound on the right, we have the following series of symbols:

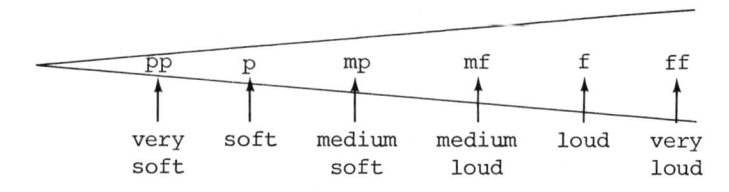

>pp   p   mp   mf   f   ff
>very   soft medium medium loud very
>soft   soft   loud   loud

Do the following exercise:

Use the Shield

The softest sound in music would be identified by using the letter _____ several times in a row.

❧
p

Which of the following symbols means "medium soft"?

>p   mp   mf   pp

❧
mp

Ranging from softest to loudest sounds, which of the following symbols are *not* in the correct order?

>(softest) pp p mf mp f ff (loudest)

❧
mf and mp are reversed.

Now return to part 37 and answer the Diagnostic Question.

===== 40 =====

Diagnostic Question Seven

Do you know the meanings of the terms crescendo and decrescendo and their accompanying symbols, $<$ and $>$? One of them means to become softer, and the other means to become louder. The following statements are either true or false:

1. Crescendo means to become louder.
2. Decrescendo means to become softer.

Alternatives

		part
a.	Both statements are true.	44
b.	Both statements are false.	43

===== 41 =====

You have made a mistake, but the following explanation should help you understand these symbols. Read on in part 39.

===== 42 =====

You've confused two of the symbols. The explanation that should clear up the problem for you is in part 39.

43

No, that was not the correct alternative. A look at the chart below should clarify the problem.

<────   soft . . . CRESCENDO   loud   DECRESCENDO . . . soft   ────>

Crescendo means TO BECOME LOUDER, and decrescendo means TO BECOME SOFTER. Decrescendo has the same prefix (de-) as decrease, and the word means TO DECREASE IN VOLUME OF SOUND.

Turn back to part 40 and see if you can answer the Diagnostic Question.

44

Correct. The prefix "de-" on decrescendo means to decrease the sound.

You have now reached the end of the first chapter. The next step is to refine your abilities by completing these activities.

Proficiency Developers

1. Clap the rhythm of the song "This Old Man" (part 45) by reading the notes and clapping the rhythm you see. Be sure to observe the rests.
2. Sing the melody of "This Old Man," using the words "long" or "ta" for quarter notes, and "short" or "te" for eighth notes.
3. Identify by name all the printed symbols in the song, including the time values of the notes and rests.

Turn to part 45.

45

THIS OLD MAN

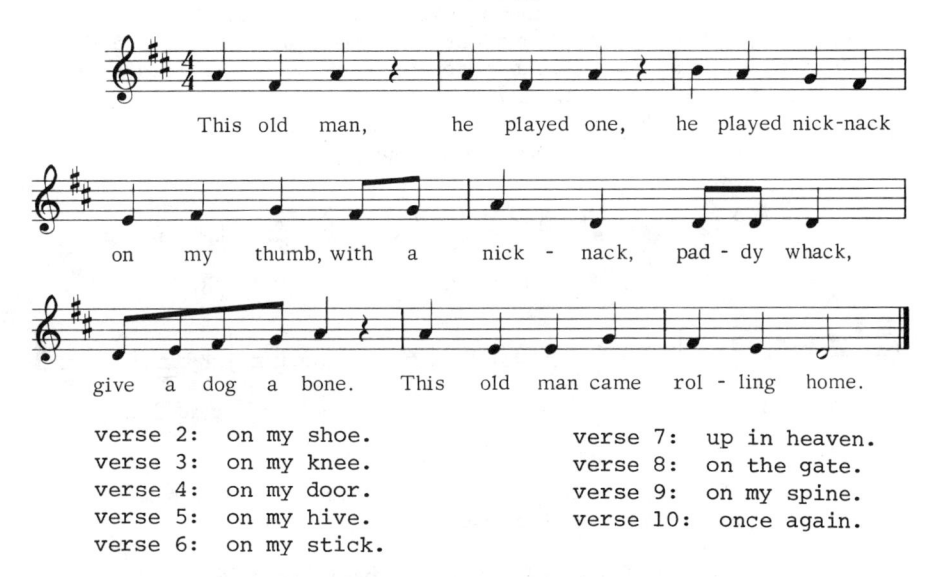

This old man, he played one, he played nick-nack on my thumb, with a nick-nack, pad-dy whack, give a dog a bone. This old man came rol-ling home.

verse 2: on my shoe.	verse 7: up in heaven.
verse 3: on my knee.	verse 8: on the gate.
verse 4: on my door.	verse 9: on my spine.
verse 5: on my hive.	verse 10: once again.
verse 6: on my stick.	

4. Copy the song "This Old Man" on the blank staff lines below. Some common errors to watch out for include (a) putting the stem on the wrong side of the note, (b) failing to write notes squarely on the line or in the space, and (c) crowding the notes together, making them difficult to read.

Turn to part 46.

5. Identify the highest and lowest notes in both songs below. Then chant each of the songs twice, first using the words of the songs, then using "long" or "ta" for quarter notes and "short" or "te" for eighth notes. Try singing all the songs you have worked with in this chapter.

GO TELL AUNT RHODY

Go tell Aunt Rho-dy, go tell Aunt Rho - dy,

Go tell Aunt Rho - dy the old gray goose is dead.

2. The one she's been saving (repeat two times)
   to make a feather bed.

3. The goslings are crying (repeat two times)
   because the goose is dead.

4. The gander is grieving (repeat two times)
   because the goose is dead.

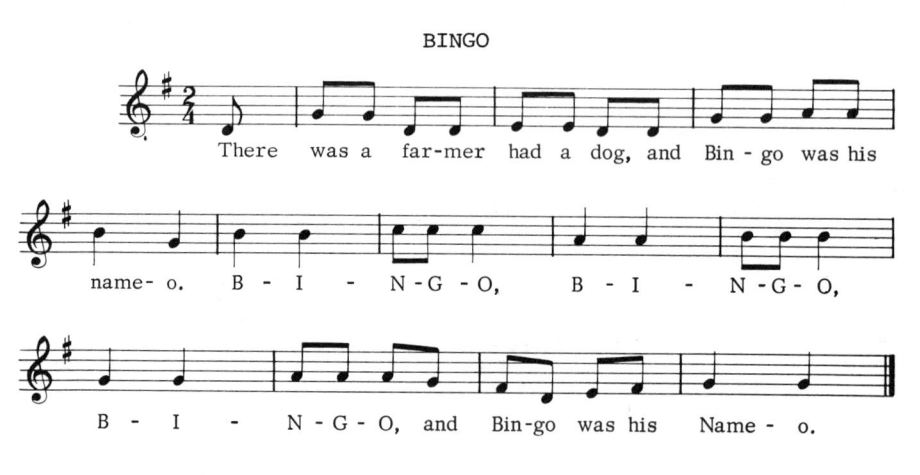

BINGO

There was a far-mer had a dog, and Bin - go was his

name- o. B - I - N-G-O, B - I - N-G-O,

B - I - N-G-O, and Bin-go was his Name - o.

Turn to part 47.

« Just for Fun »

Before you take the Self-Test, try this series of riddles.

SYMBOL ADDITION*

Determine the word for each of the musical symbols below by adding and subtracting (and possibly unscrambling) the following letters as directed.

1. EXAMPLE: FROG + AT - RAG + LATE - TOE = FROGATLATE = FLAT
2. CHIN - IN + LEFT + L - HIT = _Clef_
3. NORTH + TEA - RAT + AT - HAT = _Note_
4. STOP + FACE + FIND - COIN - PED = _Sffaf_ = staff
5. NOSE + ATE - SEE + SURE + HAL - HOSE = _Natural_
6. RATE + APE - A = _Rteape_ = Repeat
7. SHIP + HARP - HIP = _Sharp_
8. FRONT + NET + EAT - NEAT - T - N = _Froet_ = forte
9. ROSE + TONE - O - ONE = _Rest_
10. FRAME - ARM + MATE + RAM - ME = _FATFRAM_ = fermata
11. TIP + EAT - PAT = _Tie_
12. ACE + CENTAUR + R - RARE - U = _Accent_

Now match the number of the word above with its musical symbol.

_6_	‖: :‖	_10_	⌒	_3_	♩
_1._	♭	_2._	𝄢	_9_	𝄽
_7_	♯	_5._	♮	_4._	≡
_11_	♩♩	_12_	>𝆑	_8_	f

Now take the Self-Test, found in part 48.

*Used with permission, Karen Kammerer, University of Oregon, Eugene, Oregon.

48

Self-Test

On the left is a column of musical symbols and numbered blanks. At the right is a list of their names. Match each symbol with its correct name, and record the proper letter in the blank.

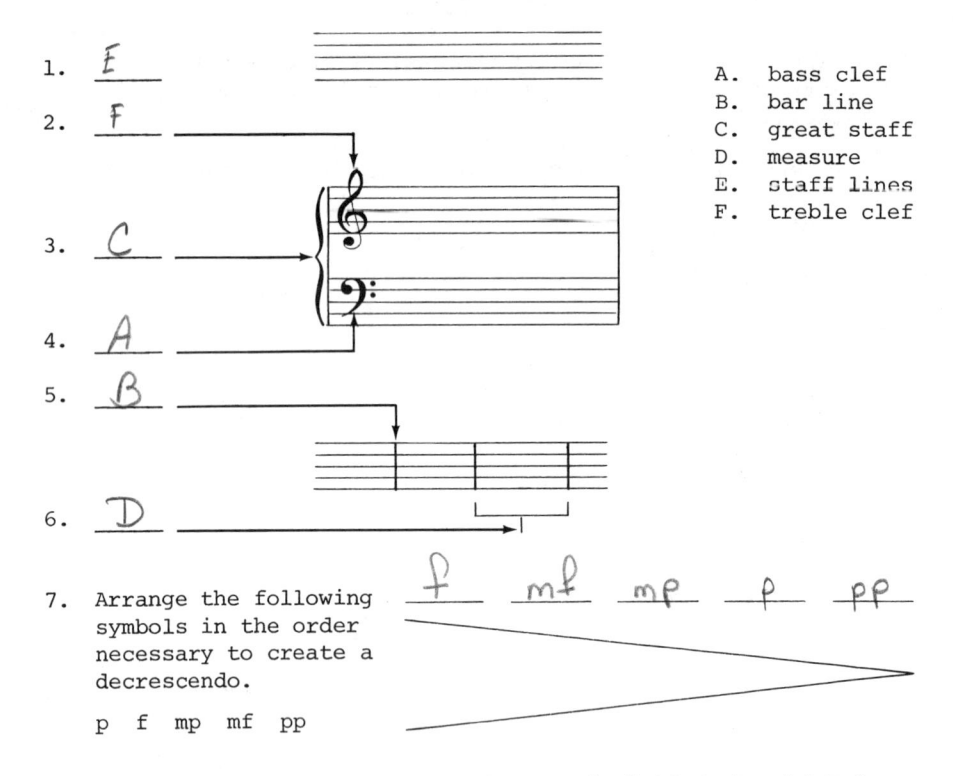

1. _E_
2. _F_
3. _C_
4. _A_
5. _B_
6. _D_

    A. bass clef
    B. bar line
    C. great staff
    D. measure
    E. staff lines
    F. treble clef

7. Arrange the following symbols in the order necessary to create a decrescendo.

    p f mp mf pp

    _f_ _mf_ _mp_ _p_ _pp_

8. Identify each of the notes *and* rests in "Old MacDonald Had a Farm" (part 49) as a whole, half, quarter, or eighth by writing the first letter of that word next to the note.

9. Describe what the D.C. al fine at the end of the third line of the song instructs you to do. _____

10. Circle the song's highest and lowest notes.

11. How many measures are there in the song?

Please turn to part 49.

OLD MACDONALD HAD A FARM

folk tune

1. Old Mac-Don-ald had a farm, E-I-E-I-O! And on this farm he had some chicks, E-I-E-I-O! With a chick, chick here and a chick, chick there, Here a chick, there a chick, ever-y where a chick, chick

2. Duck: quack, quack   3. Pig: oink, oink   4. Dog: bow, wow, etc.

Now check your answers with those in the answer key (part 50) and grade your results. If you missed a substantial number of items, you need a review of the chapter. (You should be able to finish it much faster the second time.) Regardless of your grade, IF YOU MISSED ANY QUESTIONS, it is important to review them immediately. The number of the part where you can review a missed question is shown next to the answer.

Turn to part 50.

50

Answers & Review Index

Beside each answer, the topic and part number are shown in parentheses.

1. E (staff lines 6)
2. F (treble clef 6)
3. C (great staff 6)
4. A (bass clef 6)
5. B (bar line 7)
6. D (measure 7)
7. f mf mp p pp   (dynamic levels 39)

8. line 1, treble clef: q q q q q h, q q q q
   line 1, bass clef: h h h h h h

   line 2, treble clef: h! (q) q q q q q q h
   line 2, bass clef: h q (q) h h h h

   line 3, treble clef: q q q q h (q) e e q q e e
   line 3, bass clef: h h h (h) w

   line 4, treble clef: q q h e e q e e q e e e e q q
   line 4, bass clef: w h h h h   (rhythmic values 14)

9. D.C. al fine means: Go back to the beginning of the song, and sing to the beginning of the second line, E-I-E-I-O! (D.C. 36)

10. Highest note: the notes above *E-I*.
    Lowest note: line 2, bass clef, the quarter note under *-O!*
    (pitch 22)

11. Twelve measures are printed. There are sixteen measures if you count the D.C. al fine measures twice. (measure 7)

After you have finished reviewing the questions missed, turn to part 51.

2
Notational Components of Rhythm

51

Three of the most important components of music are rhythm, melody, and harmony. This chapter is primarily concerned with rhythm.

In the preceding chapter, you learned to identify whole, half, quarter, and eighth notes, and rests. You are now going to apply your understanding of time values to more complex rhythmic concepts. Read the objectives carefully for a full understanding of what will be required of you at the end of the chapter. This chapter has eleven Diagnostic Questions.

Objectives

When you reach the end of Chapter 2, you will be asked to do the following:

1. Recognize a definition of rhythm.
2. Identify various meter (time) signatures used in music.
3. Illustrate the number of notes and the kinds of notes called for in each of the meter signatures.
4. Match measures of music with their appropriate meter signatures.
5. Identify some of the various rhythmic possibilities in a measure of music.

Most of these items relate to meter signatures and their use. You will also be asked to identify these rhythmic features of music:

1. Two ways of writing eighth and sixteenth notes.
2. Tied notes and dotted notes, and the changes in note duration they indicate.
3. Accents, legato and staccato marks, pick up notes, and slurred notes.

It is good that you took the time to read the objectives. It is a demonstrated fact that we learn better when it is clear what will be expected of us. Turn to part 52.

================ 52 ================

Diagnostic Question One

Rhythm has been defined as "the aspect of music comprising all elements that relate to forward movement." Rhythm may more simply be called a "progression of pulses or beats through time." Anyone who has danced or even tapped his foot to music has experienced this feeling of movement through time, or as it is called here, rhythm.

All but one of the following statements has something to do with rhythm. Which statement IS NOT CONCERNED with rhythm in music?

Alternatives

		part
a.	The music of a waltz has a different beat than the music of a cha-cha.	64
b.	Some pieces of music are performed much slower than others.	58
(c.)	Some songs go too high for my voice.	57

================ 53 ================

You must have overlooked something. Please turn to part 59 for an explanation.

================ 54 ================

That wasn't a poor guess, was it? An honest mistake is permissible, but you should never guess.

The question was: What two notes does this note (♩.) equal? The dotted quarter note (♩.) is equal to one and one-half the value of a quarter note. If that tip is sufficient for you to answer the Diagnostic Question correctly, return to part 65. A more detailed review begins in part 67.

55

Not quite. Here's hoping that wasn't a guess. An honest mistake is permissible, but you should never guess. The question was:

What two notes does this note (𝅘𝅥𝅮•) equal? It is a dotted quarter note, and remember, A DOT AFTER A NOTE ALWAYS INCREASES THE DURATION OF THE NOTE BY ONE HALF. If you are ready to try the question again, return to part 65. A more detailed review begins in part 67.

56

Diagnostic Question Three

Which of the following musical equations is correct throughout?

Alternatives

		part
a.	I'm not really sure which is right. May I review this concept?	59
b.	𝅗𝅥 = 𝅘𝅥 𝅘𝅥 = 𝅘𝅥𝅮 𝅘𝅥𝅮 𝅘𝅥𝅮 𝅘𝅥𝅮 or 𝅘𝅥𝅯𝅘𝅥𝅯𝅘𝅥𝅯𝅘𝅥𝅯 𝅘𝅥𝅯𝅘𝅥𝅯𝅘𝅥𝅯𝅘𝅥𝅯	63
c.	𝅗𝅥 = 𝅘𝅥 𝅘𝅥 = 𝅘𝅥𝅮 𝅘𝅥𝅮 or 𝅘𝅥𝅯𝅘𝅥𝅯	61
(d.)	𝅗𝅥 = 𝅘𝅥 𝅘𝅥 = 𝅘𝅥𝅮 𝅘𝅥𝅮 𝅘𝅥𝅮 𝅘𝅥𝅮	70

You are right. Whether a song is high or low has to do with its melody, not rhythm.

As you learned in the preceding chapter, the basic notes in music are the whole note (𝐨), half note (𝅗𝅥), quarter note (♩), eighth note (♪), and sixteenth note (𝅘𝅥𝅯). It is just as true in music as in mathematics that two halves equal one whole, or that two quarters equal one half. You are now ready for another Diagnostic Question.

Diagnostic Question Two

The mathematical relationship of music notes is illustrated on the right. Observe the two ways of writing eighth and sixteenth notes shown in the chart —with flags or with connecting beams. There is absolutely no difference in time value between two notes with flags (♪♪) and the same two notes with a beam.

Which of the following musical equations is mathematically correct?

Alternatives

		part
a.	I prefer a review of these note values.	59
b.	𝐨 = 𝅗𝅥 𝅗𝅥 = ♩♩♩♩	68
c.	𝐨 = ♩♩ = ♪♪♪♪	62
d.	𝐨 = 𝅗𝅥 𝅗𝅥 = ♪♪♪♪	53

(b is circled)

58

That isn't quite right. Here's why. You must have noticed that some songs are slower than others. If you were to tap your foot to a slow piece of music and then tap it to a fast piece, you would see that the speed of the beat changes. That change is related to rhythm. You were asked to select the response that is NOT involved with rhythmic differences. Now, see if you can choose the correct response. Return to part 52.

First, let's look at the individual notes under consideration:

𝅝 = whole note   ♩ = quarter note

𝅗𝅥 = half note   ♪ = eighth note

As you learned in arithmetic, it takes two eighths to equal one fourth. Similarly in music, two eighths equal one fourth—or one quarter note: ♪♪ = ♩ ; two fourths equal one half: ♩♩ = 𝅗𝅥 ; and two halves equal one whole: 𝅗𝅥 𝅗𝅥 = 𝅝. Therefore,

1 whole = 2 halves = 4 quarters = 8 eighths

𝅝 = 𝅗𝅥 𝅗𝅥   = ♩♩♩♩   = ♪♪♪♪ ♪♪♪♪

You can change the order of these notes, or you can leave out an entire group between the equal signs, but you may not leave out any part of a group.

Correct 𝅗𝅥 𝅗𝅥 = 𝅝 = ♩♩♩♩

Incorrect 𝅗𝅥 = 𝅝 = ♪♪♪♪ = ♩♩

A complete ratio chart looks like this:

𝅝 = 𝅗𝅥 𝅗𝅥 = ♩♩♩♩ = ♪♪♪♪ ♪♪♪♪ =
♪♪♪♪ ♪♪♪♪ ♪♪♪♪ ♪♪♪♪

Turn to part 60.

Use the Shield

Is the following example mathematically correct?   𝅝 = 𝅗𝅥 𝅗𝅥 = ♪♪♪♪

☙

No: either the last four notes should be quarter notes (♩♩♩♩) or there should be eight eighths (♪♪♪♪♪♪♪♪).

Is this example correct?   ♪♪♪♪ = 𝅗𝅥 𝅗𝅥 = 𝅝

☙

yes

How about this one? Is it correct?   ♩♩♩ = ♪♪♪♪♪♪

☙

yes

Here is one final example. Is it correct?   ♪♪♪♪♪♪♪♪ = ♩♩♩♩ = 𝅝

☙

No: either there should be two half notes at the end (𝅗𝅥 𝅗𝅥) or one whole note (𝅝).

Put the Shield Aside

By now, you may have seen that eighth notes can be written in two ways. A long series of eighth notes (♪♪♪♪♪♪♪♪) may be joined together and broken into groups (♫♫♫♫) to make it easier to recognize the number of notes in the series.

Now return to part 57 and answer the Diagnostic Question.

61

Not quite. Let me explain it briefly. The pattern you chose looks like this:

$$\text{𝅗𝅥} = \text{♩♩} = \text{♫ or ♪♪}$$

The first two units are correct: $\text{𝅗𝅥} = \text{♩♩}$. The last two units ♪♪ or ♫, are incorrect. They are eighth notes, and it takes four eighth notes to equal two quarter notes. The correct pattern looks like this:

$$\text{𝅗𝅥} = \text{♩♩} = \text{♪♪♪♪ or ♬♬}$$

If you need to review this concept further, turn to part 59.

If not, try the last question again by returning to part 56.

62

No, something was wrong with that alternative. Please turn to part 59.

63

Not quite. The pattern you chose looks like this:

$$\mathbf{o} = \mathbf{\rfloor}\mathbf{\rfloor} = \mathbf{\rfloor}\mathbf{\rfloor}\mathbf{\rfloor}\mathbf{\rfloor} \text{ or } \mathbf{\rfloor\rfloor\rfloor\rfloor}\;\mathbf{\rfloor\rfloor\rfloor\rfloor}$$

The first three parts of the example are correct:

$$\mathbf{o} = \mathbf{\rfloor}\mathbf{\rfloor} = \mathbf{\rfloor}\mathbf{\rfloor}\mathbf{\rfloor}\mathbf{\rfloor}$$

The last group of notes ♫♫♫ ♫♫♫ is incorrect.

These are eighth notes, just like the four notes in the third group. The flags have merely been written in a different way, that is, with a beam. In other words, ♪♪ and ♫ represent the same time value.

To be correct the pattern should look like this:

$$\mathbf{o} = \mathbf{\rfloor}\mathbf{\rfloor} = \mathbf{\rfloor}\mathbf{\rfloor}\mathbf{\rfloor}\mathbf{\rfloor} \text{ or } \mathbf{\rfloor\rfloor\rfloor\rfloor}$$

If you would like to review this concept further, turn to part 59.

If not, try that last question again by returning to part 56.

64

Woops, that one caught you. Why does the waltz have a different beat than the cha-cha? Because they have different rhythms. The waltz has a slow, simple rhythm in three beats: 1—2—3—. The cha-cha has a fast and complicated rhythm in four beats: 1 and, 2 and, 3 and, 4 and. Because of this difference in their beats, the two dances are rhythmically different. You were asked to choose the statement that does not involve rhythm. You should be able to choose the correct response now. Return to part 52.

65

Diagnostic Question Four

All that is new here is the dot after the note: ♩.. Don't be misled by the fact that a dotted quarter note is used as an example; you can put dots after all other notes as well.

THE DOT INCREASES A NOTE'S TIME VALUE, OR DURATION, BY ONE HALF. The dotted note is of great importance in music because, proportionately, it is equal in value to two other notes. Can you identify the two notes that are the equivalent of a dotted quarter note?

Without guessing, choose the correct alternative below.

Alternatives

		part
a.	I'm not sure of the answer, but I am willing to learn.	67
b.	♩. = ♩ + ♪	71
c.	♩. = 𝅗𝅥 + ♩	54
d.	♩. = ♪ + ♪	55

66

Correct! I'm glad you noticed that tied notes must always be on the same line or space. Otherwise they are not tied notes. These notes are connected by a tie, but the curved line between these notes is called a SLUR and is entirely different. (The slur will be explained later in the program.) The second note of two tied notes is never sounded separately. The first note is played and held for the duration of both notes without any break. As its name implies, the tie joins them together.

The next step of the program involves METER SIGNATURES. For that concept go to part 75.

67

The concept of a dotted note is not difficult to comprehend. A dot is used to increase a note's time value. In fact, A DOT ALWAYS INCREASES A NOTE'S TIME VALUE BY ONE HALF.

For example:

        Dotted whole note   = whole note   + half note
               𝅝·   =   𝅝   + 𝅗𝅥

        Dotted half note   = half note   + quarter note
               𝅗𝅥·   =   𝅗𝅥   + ♩

        Dotted quarter note = quarter note + eighth note
               ♩·   =   ♩   + ♪

        Dotted eighth note   = eighth note + sixteenth note
               ♪·   =   ♪   + 𝅘𝅥𝅯

Use the Shield

Which of the following notes has the longest time value: ♩· or 𝅗𝅥 ?

⤳

𝅗𝅥 ; a half note (𝅗𝅥) equals two quarter notes (♩ ♩), whereas a dotted quarter note (♩·) equals a quarter plus an eighth (♩+♪).

A dotted eighth note (♪·) has the same time value as what two notes?

⤳

♪· = ♪ + 𝅘𝅥𝅯

Go to part 69.

68

Correct. Let's try another, similar question to make sure you understand these relationships. Go to part 56.

69

Use the Shield

Which two notes equal a dotted half note (𝅗𝅥.)?

☙

𝅗𝅥. = 𝅗𝅥 + ♩

Is the following example correct?   𝅗𝅥. = 𝅗𝅥 + ♪

☙

yes

Is this example correct?   𝅗𝅥. = 𝅗𝅥 + ♪

☙

no: 𝅗𝅥. = 𝅗𝅥 + ♩

Now, return to part 65.

70

Very good, that was the right answer. You are ready for the next concept—the dotted note. Go to part 65.

71

Good. The dot after a note increases its time value by one half. Hence, a dotted quarter note (♩.) is equal in value to a quarter note plus an eighth note (♩ + ♪). The dot is a handy device, but sometimes it is necessary to write in the note it represents. In music, the equivalent of the mathematical plus sign is the TIE. For more on this subject, proceed with the next Diagnostic Question.

Diagnostic Question Five

In music notation when you want to use two notes to equal a dotted note, you TIE the notes. "Tied" notes are connected with a curved line: ♩♪. Remembering that a dot after a note increases its duration (time value) by one half, choose the combination of "tied" notes below that are the equivalent of a dotted quarter note.

This dotted quarter note (♩.) equals:

Alternatives

		part
a.	The two examples below look about the same to me. Please explain the difference.	74
b.		73
(c.)		66

72

You apparently need to review this question. The review is found in part 79.

73

You have made a slight mistake. Please read on in part 74.

74

Here is your explanation. There were two different curved-line symbols in the example.

slurred notes   tied notes

In the example on the left, the slur extending between notes on two DIFFERENT lines does not combine time values; it will be discussed later in the program. Only when the two notes are on the same line or space are they tied. In the example on the right, the notes are joined by a tie and have a time value equal to a dotted quarter note (♩·). In the first example, the notes are not on the same line or space. Therefore, they are not tied notes.

These measures are equal.   These measures are equal.

Write the two tied notes that are equivalent to each of the notes given on the left.

example: ♩· = ♩ ♪

(A) ♩ =

(B) ♪· =

(C) ♩· =

(D) ♩ =

ANSWERS:
(A) The half note equals two tied quarter notes.
(B) The dotted eighth equals tied eighth and sixteenth notes.
(C) The dotted half equals tied half and quarter notes.
(D) The quarter note equals tied eighth notes.

Now return to part 71 and see if you can answer the Diagnostic Question correctly.

Diagnostic Question Six

The meter signature* is found close to the clef sign, as illustrated below.

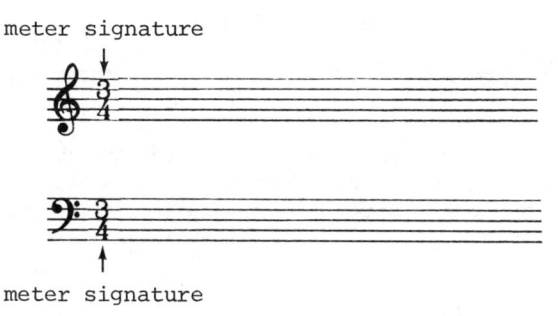

$$\text{meter signature} \downarrow$$

$$\text{(treble clef) } \frac{3}{4}$$

$$\text{(bass clef) } \frac{3}{4}$$

$$\uparrow \text{ meter signature}$$

Meter signatures may consist of many different combinations of numbers. Some of the more common ones are $\frac{4}{4}, \frac{2}{4}, \frac{3}{4}, \frac{2}{2}, \frac{6}{4}, \frac{3}{8}, \frac{6}{8}$, and $\frac{9}{8}$.

Each of the two numbers in a meter signature has an important meaning. Select the correct meaning for each number in the meter signature and choose the alternative that corresponds to your answer.

In $\frac{3}{4}$ meter, the 3 determines ___A___ and the 4 determines ___B___.

(a) how many beats are in a measure
(b) what kind of note represents the beat

Alternatives

		part
a.	I really don't know. Please tell me.	79
(b.)	The 3 determines (a) The 4 determines (b)	76
c.	The 3 determines (b) The 4 determines (a)	72

*These are frequently called time signatures, but it is also correct to refer to them as meter signatures.

76

That's absolutely right. The top number in a meter signature determines HOW MANY beats will be in each measure, and the bottom number determines WHAT KIND OF note will represent each beat. If the meter signature is $\frac{3}{4}$, there will be three beats in each measure, and each beat will be the equivalent of a quarter note.

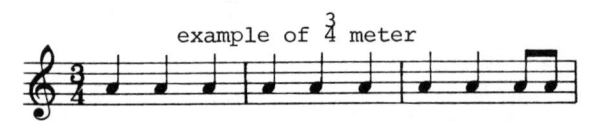

example of $\frac{3}{4}$ meter

As you see in the last measure above, two eighth notes were substituted for one quarter note. This is a perfectly legitimate substitution, and such substitutions occur very frequently in music. For example:

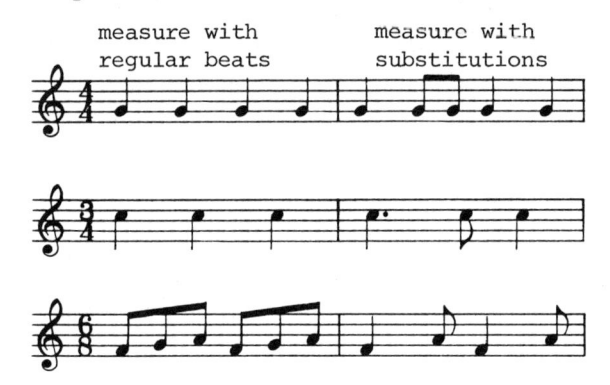

measure with regular beats   measure with substitutions

Go now to part 78.

77

Excellent. The next question will test your understanding of meter in a slightly different way. Turn to part 91.

Diagnostic Question Seven

Below are three musical examples with several substitutions in every measure. Can you determine the meter signature needed for each of the examples? Match the signatures listed at the right with the correct alternatives.

Signatures

$\frac{4}{4}$ 1.

$\frac{3}{2}$ meter

$\frac{3}{2}$ 2.

$\frac{2}{4}$ meter

$\frac{2}{4}$ 3.

$\frac{4}{4}$ meter

Alternatives

part

a. I know this step of the program is very important, and I am somewhat confused. I need a more detailed discussion. 81

(b.) 1 = $\frac{4}{4}$ meter

2 = $\frac{3}{2}$ meter

3 = $\frac{2}{4}$ meter 90

c. 1 = $\frac{2}{4}$ meter

2 = $\frac{3}{2}$ meter

3 = $\frac{4}{4}$ meter 82

d. 1 = $\frac{3}{2}$ meter

2 = $\frac{4}{4}$ meter

3 = $\frac{2}{4}$ meter 80

79

The explanation is simple.

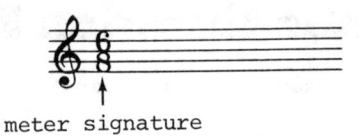

meter signature

In the above example, the meter is six-eight. A piece of music is frequently said to be in six-eight time or six-eight meter.

Six-eight meter means there are six eighth notes (or their equivalent) in each measure.

Three-four meter means there are three quarter notes in each measure.

Four-four meter means there are four quarter notes in each measure.

In other words, the top number of the meter signature determines HOW MANY beats per measure, and the bottom number determines WHAT KIND of note represents the beat.

6 → how many notes per measure
8 → what kind of note gets the beat

With this information, see if you can answer the question in part 75.

80

You have not selected the proper alternative. To clear up the problem, carefully read the material in part 81.

81

O.K., let's consider the matter a minute. Beside the clef sign on the staff below is a meter signature.

The bottom number of the meter signature determines WHAT KIND of note will be the basic beat of the measure. In three-four meter, for example, the basic beat will be the quarter note.

The top number determines HOW MANY of these notes will be represented in each measure. Music in $\frac{3}{4}$ meter will have the equivalent of three quarter notes in each measure. In short,

$\frac{3}{4}$ meter = 3 quarter notes (or their equivalent) per measure.

$\frac{6}{8}$ meter = 6 eighth notes (or their equivalent) per measure.

$\frac{4}{4}$ meter = 4 quarter notes (or their equivalent) per measure.

$\frac{3}{2}$ meter = 3 half notes (or their equivalent) per measure.

$\frac{9}{8}$ meter = 9 eighth notes (or their equivalent) per measure.

Please turn to part 83.

82

You've made a mistake, but we can now try to clear the matter up. Go on to part 81.

83

Use the Shield

With this meter signature the basic beat of the measure will be the _____ note.

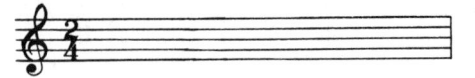

∽

quarter (indicated by the 4)

The staff at the right is an example of _____ meter.

∽

3/4 (3 quarter notes per measure)

This staff is an example of _____ meter.

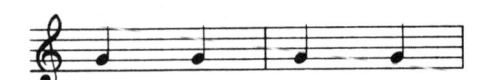

∽

2/4 (2 quarter notes per measure)

Here is an example of _____ meter.

∽

6/8 (6 eighth notes per measure)

Put the Shield Aside

When a meter signature designates that a measure is in three-four meter, we have the following possible simple construction:

Many variations are also possible. Here are three:

Turn to part 84.

84

Each of the previous examples contained the equivalent of three quarter notes (and three beats) per measure. If each of the quarter notes were converted to eighth notes, the measure would appear:

Notice how three beats are delineated by the way the beams connecting the eighth notes are grouped.

Another meter, $^6_8$, may have the same number of eighth notes per measure, but they are grouped differently. In this example, the eighth notes are grouped into two units, or beats, instead of three. Each beat is the equivalent of a dotted quarter note (♩.). This division into three beats or two beats per measure marks a fundamental difference between $^3_4$ meter and $^6_8$ meter.

Use the Shield

Does the following measure have the correct number of beats?

no (there is an extra eighth note)

Does this measure have the correct number of beats?

yes

Which measure below is INCORRECT?

measure 3 (it needs another eighth note)

Go on to part 85.

85

At first glance, you might think it difficult to determine the meter signature for the example below, but it is relatively easy.

The first two notes in the measure are eighth notes. Together they equal one quarter note. The next four notes are sixteenth notes—because of the double beam on their stems. Four sixteenth notes also equal one quarter note. Each pair of eighth notes at the end of the measure is like the one at the start. Each equals one quarter note. Thus, the measure has the equivalent of four quarter notes, as in four-four meter.

Use the Shield

Below are a musical sample and three meter signatures. Which signature is the correct one for this music?

$\frac{4}{4}$, $\frac{6}{8}$, $\frac{3}{4}$

❦

$\frac{4}{4}$

Which signature belongs with this sample?

$\frac{4}{4}$, $\frac{6}{8}$, $\frac{3}{4}$

❦

$\frac{3}{4}$

Which signature is the correct one here?

$\frac{4}{4}$, $\frac{6}{8}$, $\frac{3}{4}$

❦

$\frac{4}{4}$

Return to the Diagnostic Question in part 78.

===== 86 =====

Diagnostic Question Eight

Determine the proper meter signature for each of the following examples, and select the corresponding alternative from those given below.

Alternatives

		part
a.	If I am really honest with myself, I think a review is necessary for me to understand this question.	81
b.	1 = $\frac{4}{4}$; 2 = $\frac{3}{4}$; 3 = $\frac{4}{4}$	88
(c.)	1 = $\frac{3}{4}$; 2 = $\frac{6}{8}$; 3 = $\frac{4}{4}$	77
d.	1 = $\frac{3}{4}$; 2 = $\frac{2}{4}$; 3 = $\frac{6}{8}$	92

===== 87 =====

Sorry, your response was not accurate. You will find an explanation of this question in part 97.

88

You need to take another look at the question. Read the explanation in part 89.

89

The three examples were:

Each measure in this example has the equal of 3 quarter notes:

[musical notation with counts: 1 2 3 12]   meter signature: 3/4

This example has the equivalent of 6 eighth notes per measure:

[musical notation with counts: 1 2 3 4 5 6]   meter signature: 6/8

The equivalent of 4 quarter notes per measure is in this example:

[musical notation with counts: 1 2 3 4]   meter signature: 4/4

If you are still the least bit unsure, read the complete review in part 81.

If not, choose the correct response for the Diagnostic Question in part 86.

90

Right. You have taken a successful step toward the completion of this chapter by correctly identifying these meter signatures. Let's try another, similar problem to double-check your understanding of the important concept of meter. Go to part 86.

91

Diagnostic Question Nine

The meter signature in the example below is $\frac{3}{8}$. There should be the equivalent of three eighth notes in each measure. Which measure is not correct?

Alternatives

		part
a.	I don't know. Please explain.	97
b.	Measure 1 is incorrect.	87
c.	Measure 2 is incorrect.	104
d.	Measure 3 is incorrect.	101
e.	Measure 4 is incorrect.	96

92

That was not quite right. For an explanation of this question, go to part 89.

93

You chose the wrong alternative, but we can clear this up very quickly. Please turn to the explanation in part 103.

94

Not quite. Please read on in part 99.

95

Diagnostic Question Ten

Each example below has one incomplete measure. In which example is the incomplete measure acceptable?

[Musical examples 1, 2, and 3]

Alternatives

		part
a.	I am not sure; I would like an explanation of this concept.	103
b.	Example 1	98
c.	Example 2	93
(d.)	Example 3	100

96

That alternative can't be right. When you add a quarter note and an eighth note, you have the equivalent of three eighth notes—just what the meter signature called for. For a complete explanation go to part 97.

The meter was $\frac{3}{8}$. Any combination of notes equal to three eighth notes would be correct. You were to find the incorrect measure.

Measure 1 has this pattern: ♪♪♪. The two sixteenth notes are equal to one eighth note. When totaled, the measure contains the equivalent of three eighth notes. It is therefore correct.

In measure 2, this pattern is found: ♩.♪. The quarter note equals two eighth notes, and the dot after it equals another eighth note, for a total of three eighths. There is a sixteenth note left in the measure which is not needed; the measure is, therefore, incorrect.

Measure 3 has the following note pattern: ♪♪♪♪. Each pair of sixteenth notes equals one eighth note, so the measure is complete and correct.

Measure 4 contains one quarter note and one eighth note: ♩♪. The quarter note equals two eighth notes, plus the eighth note equals three eighth notes. The measure is correct as it stands.

Now return to part 91.

98

You have made a mistake, so let's reconsider the question. Go to part 103.

99

Here is an explanation.

1. Staccato: This term is applied to notes that are to be shortened slightly, so that the tones are separated from each other. Staccato is indicated by a dot above the note.

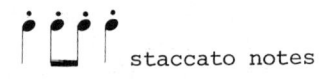

    staccato notes

2. Tenuto: This term is applied to notes that are to be lengthened slightly. The mark is merely a line above the note, showing that the tone should be stretched out somewhat.

    tenuto note

3. Slur: This symbol connects a series of notes. It serves basically the same purpose as the tenuto mark, but it is used when more than one tone is to be lengthened.

    slurred notes

4. Accent: An accent mark is used when one note is to be played or sung louder than the others around it.

    accented note

Now return to part 102.

100

You are right! An incomplete measure is allowed at the beginning of a piece of music. The extra notes are called PICKUP notes. One well-known example is our national anthem, which begins with two pickup notes on the word "Oh."

pickup notes

Oh____ say can you see by the
3   1   2   3   1 2   3

The music begins on the third beat.

Although incomplete measures are permitted at the beginning of a piece of music, they are never permitted in the middle. In fact, to make all measures equal, the extra beat of the pickup note is usually borrowed from the last measure.

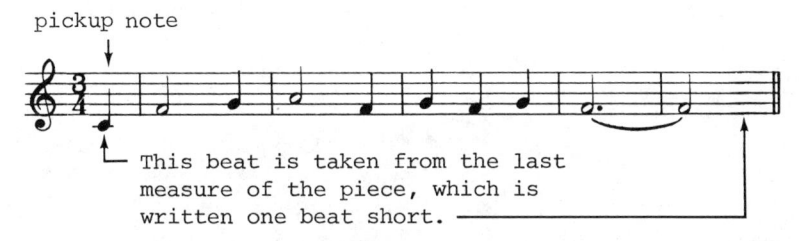

pickup note

— This beat is taken from the last measure of the piece, which is written one beat short. —

Two more examples of pickup notes follow, with numbers below the notes to show how they are counted.

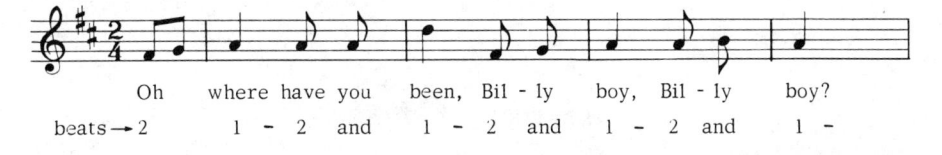

Oh   where have you   been, Bil - ly boy, Bil - ly   boy?
beats→ 2   1 - 2 and   1 - 2 and   1 - 2 and   1 -

The far - mer in the dell,____ The far - mer in the dell,___
beats→ 6   1-2-3 4-5-6 1-2-3-4-5-6   1-2-3 4-5-6 1-2-3-4-5

Now go to part 102.

101

You have made a simple mistake, but not enough to be overly worried about. Let's study it for a minute in part 97.

102

Diagnostic Question Eleven

You have now reached the last Diagnostic Question in this chapter. To answer it correctly, please read carefully.

In the three columns below, the first lists musical terms; the second shows the musical symbols used in their places; and the third column defines the symbols.

Match the three columns (your answer will be something like A-1-X or B-2-Y) and find your answer in the alternatives below.

Musical Terms	Symbols	Explanations
A. staccato	1. (four slurred notes)	W. separate the notes
B. tenuto	2. (note with dash)	X. lengthen the note
C. slur	3. (note with dot)	Y. stress this note
D. accent	4. (note with accent)	Z. connect the notes

Alternatives

		part
a.	These words are strange to me. I would like an explanation.	99
b.	A-3-W B-2-X C-1-Z D-4-Y	105
c.	A-3-W B-4-Y C-1-X D-2-Z	94

103

You were asked if an incomplete measure is acceptable in the first measure, anywhere in the middle, or at the end of a piece.

INCOMPLETE MEASURES ARE ACCEPTABLE ONLY AT THE BEGINNING OF A PIECE OF MUSIC, AND AT THE END OF A PIECE THAT BEGINS WITH AN INCOMPLETE MEASURE. The notes in those incomplete measures that begin a piece are called PICKUP NOTES. Many well-known songs have pickup notes in them. Look at "Dixie" for example:

pickup notes

I ___ wish I was_ in the land of cot-ton

Another example of a pickup note is the beginning of the well-known song "Auld Lang Syne":

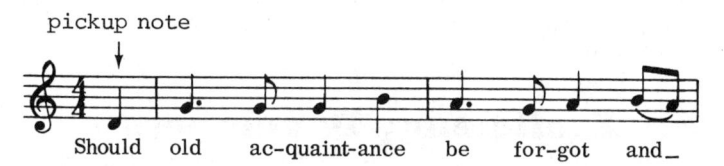

pickup note

Should old ac-quaint-ance be for-got and_

Now, return to the Diagnostic Question in part 95.

104

Correct! You are doing very well. In fact, you don't have much further to go in this chapter. Take a deep breath so your mind is sharp and clear. Then answer the Diagnostic Question in part 95.

105

That's right!

1. Staccato notes (𝄾𝄾) are to be separated from each other.

2. Tenuto notes (𝄾) are to be lengthened slightly.

3. Slurred notes (🎵🎵🎵🎵) are to be connected. If only two notes are slurred (♩♩), they must be different tones or they would be TIED notes.

4. Accented notes (𝄾) are to be stressed or emphasized more than the notes around them.

Congratulations! You are now at the end of chapter 2. Please do the following exercises; they will help you use the knowledge you have just acquired.

Proficiency Developers

1. On the staff below, draw two notes that are tied. Then draw two notes joined by a slur.

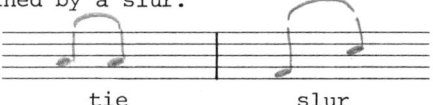

    tie   slur

2. Change the quarter notes below into eighth notes by adding flags or beams as indicated.

    flags   beams

3. Identify the meter of each of the following measures:

Please turn to part 106.

4. Write a definition of musical rhythm in the space provided below:

A progression of pulses or beats through time.

5. Which musical sample below is in $\frac{6}{8}$ meter? Which is in $\frac{3}{4}$ meter?

6. How can you tell the difference between $\frac{6}{8}$ and $\frac{3}{4}$ meter?

7. The following song has no meter signature or bar lines. It should be sung in a simple flowing rhythm with pauses where the fermatas occur. Try singing it several times and notice the unique feeling of music without prescribed meter.

O COME, O COME, EMMANUEL

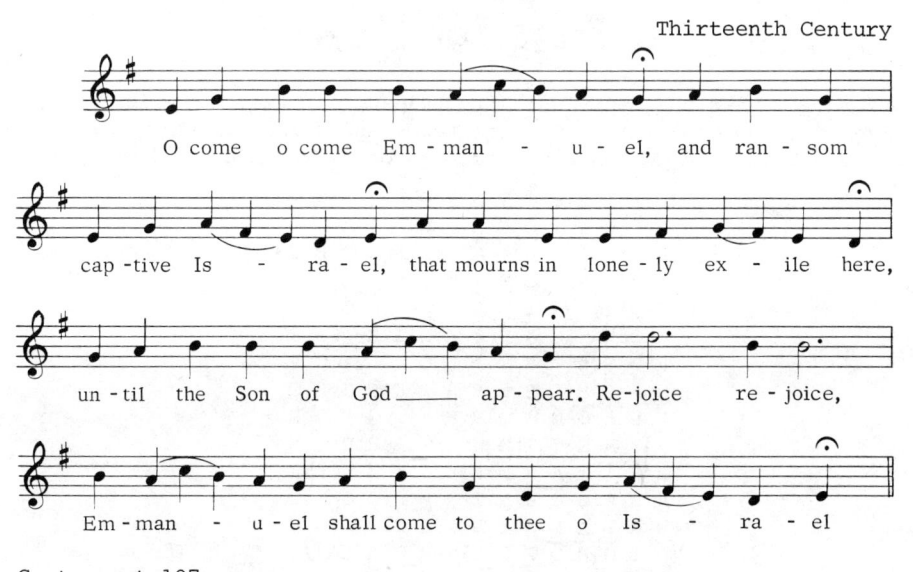

Thirteenth Century

O come o come Em - man - u - el, and ran - som cap -tive Is - ra - el, that mourns in lone - ly ex - ile here, un -til the Son of God ap - pear. Re-joice re - joice, Em - man - u - el shall come to thee o Is - ra - el

Go to part 107.

8. In the song "Yankee Doodle" locate all the dotted notes. Clap the rhythm of the song, being careful to perform the dotted notes accurately. Then sing it.

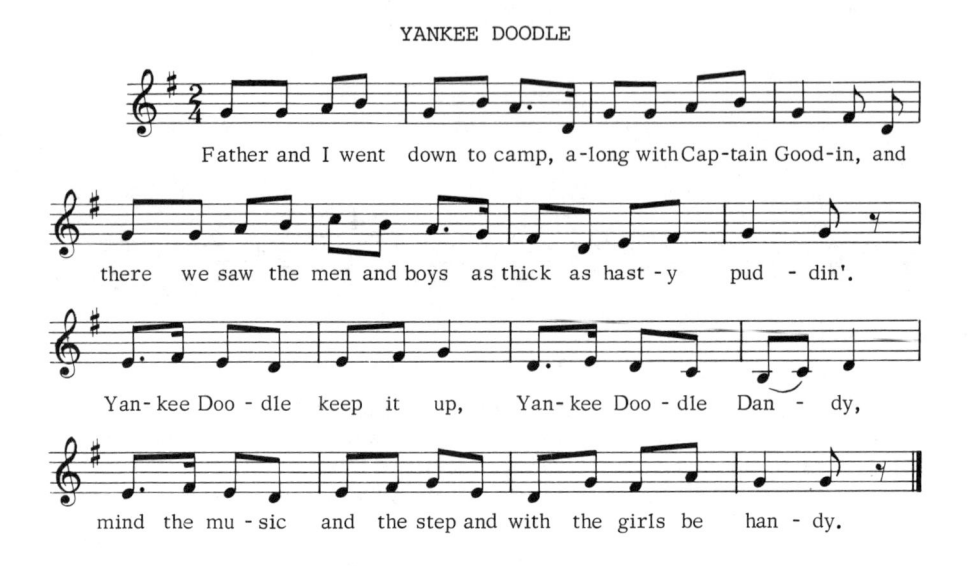

YANKEE DOODLE

Father and I went down to camp, a-long with Cap-tain Good-in, and there we saw the men and boys as thick as hast-y pud-din'. Yan-kee Doo-dle keep it up, Yan-kee Doo-dle Dan-dy, mind the mu-sic and the step and with the girls be han-dy.

« Just for Fun »

Before you take the Self-Test, try this word puzzle. Hidden in the diagram below are over 35 musical terms and symbols. Circle all you can find, and remember to look up, down, and from either side.*

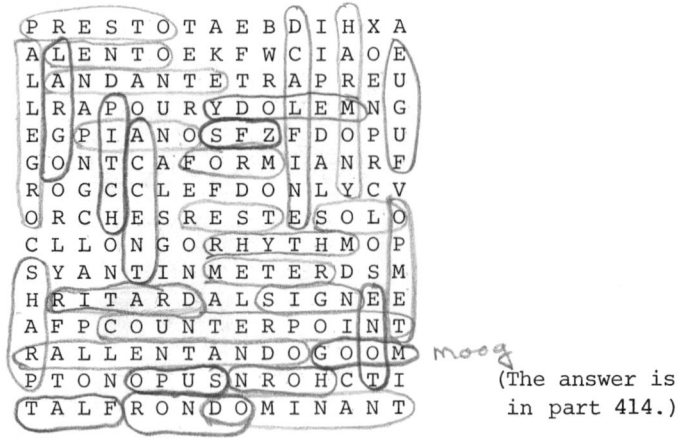

```
P R E S T O T A E B D I H X A
A L E N T O E K F W C I A O E
L A N D A N T E T R A P R E U
L R A P O U R Y D O L E M N G
E G P I A N O S F Z F D O P U
G O N T C A F O R M I A N R F
R O G C C L E F D O N L Y C V
O R C H E S R E S T E S O L O
C L L O N G O R H Y T H M O P
S Y A N T I N M E T E R D S M
H R I T A R D A L S I G N E E
A F P C O U N T E R P O I N T
R A L L E N T A N D O G O O M
P T O N O P U S N R O H C T I
T A L F R O N D O M I N A N T
```

(The answer is in part 414.)

Go to part 108.

*Used with permission, Karen Kammerer, University of Oregon, Eugene, Oregon.

Self-Test

1. "Farmer in the Dell" has been printed below without bar lines, except for the first measure. Fill in the remaining bar lines for the complete song.

FARMER IN THE DELL

The far-mer in the dell,___ the far-mer in the dell,___
Heigh - ho, the der - ry oh, the far - mer in the dell.___

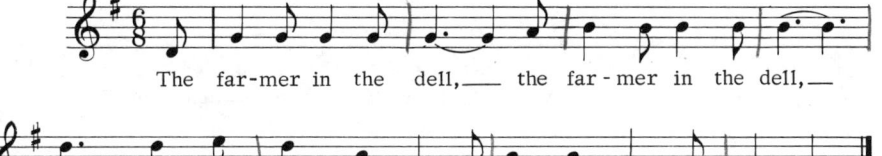

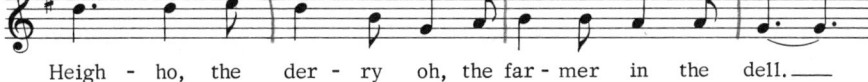

    2: The farmer takes a wife.
    3: The wife takes a child.
    4: The child takes a dog.
    5: The dog takes a cat.
    6: The cat takes a mouse.
    7: The mouse takes some cheese.
    8: The cheese stands alone.

Please turn to part 109.

2. "Little Tom Tinker" has been printed below without bar lines, except for the first measure. Write in the remaining bar lines for the complete song.

LITTLE TOM TINKER

Lit - tle Tom Tin - ker sat down on a clink - er and he be - gan to cry,___ Ma!___ Ma!___ Poor lit - tle in - no - cent guy.___

3. On what words in "Farmer in the Dell" or "Little Tom Tinker" is a SLUR employed? *Ma!*

4. On what words in either song is a TIE employed? *dell / guy*

5. What beat does the pickup note get in "Farmer in the Dell"? *6*

6. Which measure below has the INCORRECT number of noted in it?

1
2
(3)
4

Please turn to part 110.

110

On the left are a series of dotted notes and tied notes. On the right, mathematical equivalents of each example are listed randomly. Select a letter for each number and write it in the proper blank.

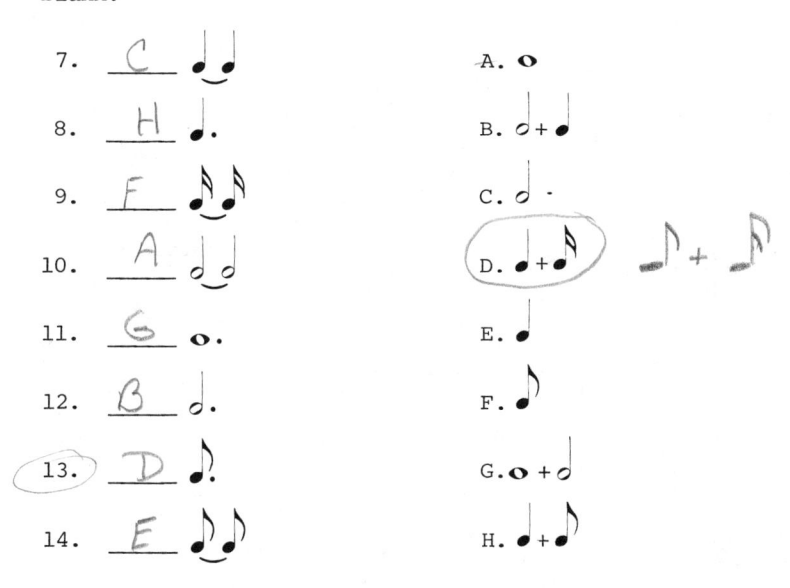

7. __C__ ♩♩
8. __H__ ♩.
9. __F__ ♪♪
10. __A__ ♩♩
11. __G__ o.
12. __B__ ♩.
13. __D__ ♪.
14. __E__ ♪♪

A. o
B. o + ♩
C. ♩ ·
D. ♩ + ♪
E. ♩
F. ♪
G. o + ♩
H. ♩ + ♩

For the six music samples below, choose the proper meter signature shown at the right and record your answer.

15. 2/4
16. 3/4
17. 6/8
18. 6/4 (3/2)
19. 4/4
20. 3/8

Please turn to part 111.

111

Match the expression marks on the left with the proper definition from the right.

21. _C_ ♩̄   A. staccato note: to be separated from other notes and shortened.

22. _D_ ♩>   B. tied quarter notes: equal to one half note.

23. _A_ ♩̇   C. tenuto note: to be lengthened slightly.

24. _B_ ♩‿♩   D. accented note: to be played louder than the surrounding notes.

YOU HAVE NOW COMPLETED THE SELF TEST

Check your answers with the key that follows and grade your results. If you missed a substantial number of the items, you should read the chapter again before going on. In any case, be sure to review each question you missed before proceeding. (The signal ff indicates the review continues to other parts.)

Turn to part 112.

Answers & Review Index

1. "Farmer in the Dell." Put bar lines in the following places: line one: before the word *dell*, before *far-mer*, before *dell*, after *dell*. (meter signatures 81 ff) line two: before *der-ry*, before *far-mer*, before *dell*.

2. "Little Tom Tinker." Put bar lines in the following places: line one: before the word *he*, before *cry*, after the rest following *cry*. (meter signatures 81 ff) line two: before the second *ma*, before *poor*, before *guy*.

3. In "Little Tom Tinker," line two, the words *ma, ma*. (slur and tie 74)

4. In "Farmer in the Dell," the word *dell* employs a tie three times.
In "Little Tom Tinker," on the words *cry* and *guy*. (slur and tie 74)

5. The sixth (last) count of the measure. (pickup notes 103)

6. Measure 3 (meter signatures 81 ff)

7. C (tied notes 74)

8. H (dotted notes 67)

9. F (tied notes 74)

10. A (tied notes 74)

11. G (dotted notes 67)

12. B (dotted notes 67)

13. D (dotted notes 67)

14. E (tied notes 74)

15. $\frac{2}{4}$ meter (meter signatures 81 ff)

16. $\frac{3}{4}$ meter (meter signatures 81 ff)

17. $\frac{6}{8}$ meter (meter signatures 81 ff)

18. $\frac{6}{4}$ meter (meter signatures 81 ff)

19. $\frac{4}{4}$ meter (meter signatures 81 ff)

Please continue on the following page.

20. $\frac{3}{8}$ meter (meter signatures 81 ff)
21. C (tenuto mark 99)
22. D (accented note 99)
23. A (staccato note 99)
24. B (tied notes 74)

3
Notational Components of Melody

113

Music as we know it seldom consists of rhythm alone. It also includes MELODY, the subject of this chapter. You will recall from chapter 1 how to locate the highest and lowest notes in a passage of music. Now it is time to consider all the notes on a staff, how the staff is used as a framework for notating melody, and how the staff is related to a piano keyboard. A system of organizing notes, or tones, into scales based on a particular key tone will also be introduced.

Objectives

At the conclusion of this chapter, you will be asked to demonstrate your knowledge of the music staff by:

1. Recognizing a definition of pitch.
2. Recalling the names of notes on the treble staff.
3. Recalling the names of notes on the bass staff.
4. Matching the symbols for sharps, flats, and naturals with their proper descriptions.
5. Identifying an octave on the staff.
6. Recognizing ledger lines.

Using a replica of the piano keyboard, you will be asked to do the following:

1. Recall from memory the names of the notes of the white keys.
2. Demonstrate an understanding of the relationship between sharps and flats and the black keys.
3. Identify an octave on the piano keyboard.

You will be introduced to the concept of a major scale and will be required to do the following:

(Please continue on the following page.)

1. Identify whole steps and half steps.
2. Recognize the places in the major scale where half steps are located.
3. Recognize the definition of a key signature.
4. Identify a key signature.
5. Recognize the key signatures for the keys of C-major, G-major, E-major, B♭-major, and D-major.

In this chapter there are fifteen Diagnostic Questions.

Turn to part 114.

114

Diagnostic Question One*

The highness or lowness of a tone is called its PITCH. As you learned earlier, the pitch of a note is determined by its placement on the staff. The higher it is placed on the staff, the higher its pitch; the lower it is on the staff, the lower its pitch.

Notes can be placed on any line or any space of the staff, depending on the pitch desired. Each of these lines and spaces has a letter name—A, B, C, D, E, F, or G. After the G, the pitches start over again with A. There is no such note as H.

Can you identify the notes of the treble clef on the staff below? If so, choose the alternative that properly identifies all the notes from left to right. Then turn to the part indicated.

Alternatives

		part
a.	I'm not familiar with this aspect of music. Please explain it.	116
b.	C G A E D	122
c.	B G F E D	129
d.	B F G D C	135

115

You are right. For your next question go to part 133.

*If you have already answered the question once, correctly answer it again and continue the program as directed.

The names of the notes on the treble staff are easy to learn once you understand the system for naming lines and spaces of the staff. We'll start with the note MIDDLE C—found on a ledger line between the treble and the bass clef.

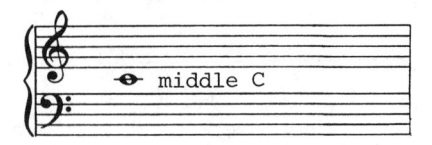

The middle C line serves the same purpose as the other lines of the staff. The space above it is D, and the notes continue to rise on the staff in alphabetical order: C, D, E, F, G. After G, the musical alphabet starts over again with A (see example below).

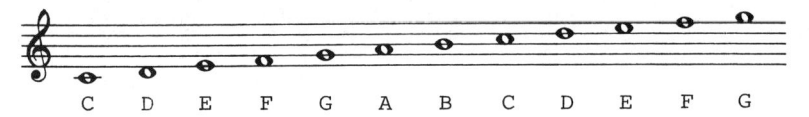

Notice that every line and every space is given a note.

Use the Shield

This note, because it is between the treble and bass clefs, is called middle _____ .

☙

C

The note directly above middle C is _____ .

☙

D

The fourth note above middle C is called _____ .

☙

G

Go to part 117.

117

Use the Shield

After G, the letters start over again with _____ .

❦

A

This note is called _____ .

❦

D

An easy way to remember the names of the spaces is to notice the word they spell when read from bottom to top.

From bottom to top, the spaces spell the word _____ .

F A C E

❦

FACE

Once you know the names of the spaces you can figure out the names of the other notes.
From left to right, these notes are _____ , _____ , and _____ .

❦

F, A, and G

Turn to part 119.

118

You are apparently confused about the notes. Did you check the name of each one? A brief review of the note names for the bass clef can be found in part 121.

119

Use the Shield

These notes are ____ ,
____ , and ____ .

~

E, D, F (E is the last space and, therefore, the last letter in the word FACE.)

What word do these notes spell?

~

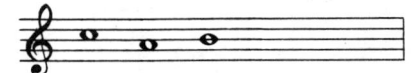

CAB

What word do these notes spell?

~

AGE

Do these two notes have the same name? What are their names?

~

Yes: They are both C, and the lower one is called middle C.

These notes tell you what many people like to do. They like to ____ .

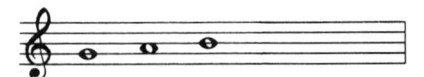

~

GAB

Turn to part 136.

120

You seem to have confused the notes. You will find the explanation you need in part 128.

121

Sorry, but this explanation should help you avoid another mistake.

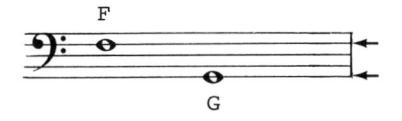

The two notes on the staff at the right are important ones for you to memorize immediately. Notice the two dots in the bass clef sign and the line between. Notes on that line are always named F.

The other important note—on the bottom line of the staff—is always called G. By remembering the names of these two notes, you can determine the other notes in the bass clef. For example, a note on the space right above G would be A. (Remember, notes go from A to G and then start over with A.)

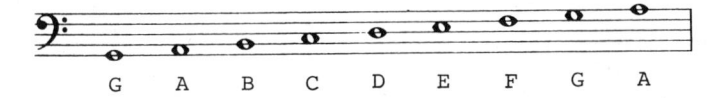

G A B C D E F G A

Be sure to assign a note to every line and every space. By being careful not to skip a line or a space, and by remembering the two key notes in the example at the top of the page, you will find it easy to recall the notes of the bass clef.

If you would like to do a short exercise on the bass clef, turn to part 130. If not, return to the question in part 133.

122

The alternative you selected was not quite right. Take a close look at the notes on the staff below. The note on the first line below the staff is middle C.

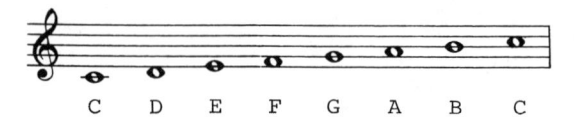

```
    C   D   E   F   G   A   B   C
```

After middle C, the notes go up alphabetically, falling alternately on each line and each space, to G. Then, they start over again with A and continue as before. Here is a speedy way to remember the notes of the treble clef:

1. Learn middle C and the space above it (D).

2. Learn the names of the spaces, from the bottom to the top. (They spell the word FACE.)

3. If you need to identify a line, determine what the space directly below it is named, and then go up alphabetically.

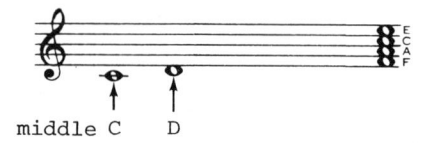

    middle C D

If a short drill on the notes of the treble clef will help fix them in your mind, go to part 116. If you are sure that you know the notes, return to part 114.

Diagnostic Question Two

What are the names of the notes on this staff?

Alternatives

		part
a.	I need to review this concept.	116
b.	E F A G F E D	124
(c.)	E G D C B A F	131
d.	G B F E D C A	140

124

You seem to be confused and in need of an explanation on the notes of the treble clef. Go on to part 125.

125

The note on the first line below the staff is middle C.

C   D   E   F   G   A   B   C   D   E   F

After middle C, the notes go up the staff alphabetically, falling alternately on lines and spaces. After G (the second line of the treble clef), the notes start over alphabetically with A and continue as before.

A speedy way to remember the notes of the treble clef is to use the following steps:

1. Learn middle C and the note (D) in the space directly above it.

2. Learn the names of the spaces, from the bottom to the top. They spell the word FACE.

3. When you need to identify a line, first determine the letter name of the space directly under under it and then go up alphabetically.

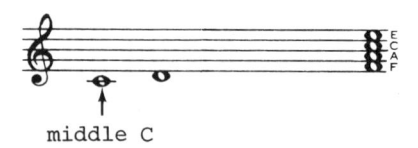

    F
    E
    C
    A
    F

    ↑
    middle C

If you would like a detailed exercise now, turn to part 116.
If you don't think you need the exercise, return to part 123 and answer the Diagnostic Question.

126

Diagnostic Question Three*

The lines and spaces of the bass clef do not have the same names as those in the treble clef. In the example below are several notes in the bass clef. Can you identify the notes and select the corresponding alternative from those listed?

Alternatives

		part
a.	I don't know the notes of the bass clef. Where is an explanation?	128
b.	G B C D E G	141
(c.)	G D E F G B	115
d.	A C D E F B	120

127

Very good!

1. The sharp (♯) raises a note by one half step.

2. The flat (♭) lowers a note by one half step.

3. The natural (♮) cancels the effect of previous sharps and flats.

4. Ledger lines are used when the pitch is so high or so low that the note must be written above or below the staff.

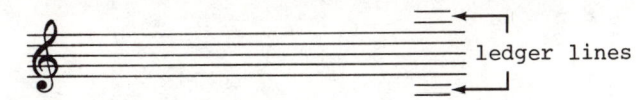

ledger lines

Now go to part 142.

*If you have already answered the question once, correctly answer it again, and continue the program.

128

Notes in the bass clef are alphabetical, just like the treble clef. They also go from A through G and then begin over with A. However, they must be learned separately because they fall on different lines and spaces of the staff.

The first two notes you need to learn are F and G.

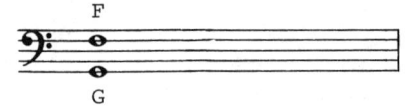

In the example, observe the bass clef sign with its two dots, and the staff line between the dots. THE LINE BETWEEN THE DOTS OF THE BASS CLEF SIGN IS ALWAYS CALLED F. Thus, the note you see on that line is F.

The second note you need to remember is on the bottom line of the staff—the G line. Memorize these two notes, and from them you can figure out all other notes in the bass clef. For example, a note on the bottom space (right above G) would be A. (Remember, notes go from A to G and then start over with A.) All the notes in the bass clef are shown below.

G A B C D E F G A B C

Turn to part 130.

129

No, you started out right on B, but the other notes were incorrect. For an explanation, go to part 116.

130

Use the Shield

Probably the easiest note to learn in the bass clef is found on the line between the dots of the bass clef sign. That note is ___ .

☙

F

Another important note in the bass clef is found on the bottom line. That note is ___ .

☙

G

Counting one note for each line and one note for each space above G, this note is found to be ___ .

☙

C

In both the treble and bass clefs, notes are named A, B, C, D, E, F, G. The note after G is always ___ .

☙

A

This note is on the space directly under F. It is named ___ .

☙

E

These two important notes of the bass clef are ___ and ___ .

☙

F, G

From left to right, these notes spell a word. What is the word?

☙

FAD

Turn to part 132.

131

Right. You have again identified the notes in the treble clef correctly. Now go to part 126.

132

Use the Shield

From left to right, what word do these notes spell?

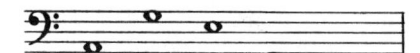

~

AGE

Do these three notes spell a word?

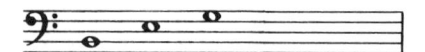

~

Yes, BEG

These notes do not spell a word. What are their names?

~

A, F, G, and C

What long word do these notes spell?

~

BAGGAGE

If you feel the need for more review, reread the material that begins in part 128. If not, return to part 126.

133

Diagnostic Question Four

Now try this longer series of notes in the bass clef. Name the notes in the following example.

Alternatives

		part
a.	I could use a review.	128
(b.)	G E B C A G C	137
c.	G E B C A F C	121
d.	G E C B A G C	118

134

The answer you chose indicates you should review these symbols.

A-SHARP (♯) RAISES A NOTE ONE HALF STEP. For example, note number 1 below is A, and note number 2 is A-SHARP. A-sharp is one half step above A, and, thus, is halfway between A and B.

```
    1    2    3    4    5
    A    A♯   B    B♭   B♮
```

A FLAT (♭) LOWERS A NOTE BY ONE HALF STEP. Note number 3 is B. Number 4 is B-flat. B-flat is one half step below B, and is halfway between A and B. In other words, B-flat and A-sharp have the same sound, but appear different on the printed page.

THE NATURAL (♮) CANCELS THE EFFECT OF ANY PREVIOUS SHARPS OR FLATS. Note number 5 needs a natural sign to indicate you are to discontinue playing the flat which was placed before note number 4.

If a note is too high (or too low) to be written on the five-line staff, we can extend the staff by adding short lines where needed. These short lines are called LEDGER LINES.

staff lines ≡≡≡≡≡≡≡≡≡≡≡ ledger lines

Now return to the Diagnostic Question in part 138.

135

Right. Let's see if you can do as well with the next musical example. Turn to part 123.

136

Use the Shield

These notes spell
_____ .

༄

BADGE

Here is a longer one.
The word is _____ .

༄

CABBAGE

These notes spell
_____ .

༄

DEED

These letters do not spell
a word. The notes are
___, ___, ___, ___, ___ .

༄

C, D, G, F, B

Now return to part 114 and see if you can answer the Diagnostic Question.

137

Good. The next question will test your knowledge of some musical symbols that are used on the staff. Please continue in part 138.

138

Diagnostic Question Five

The column on the left shows some musical symbols. The center column lists their names in a different order. The right column states the purpose of each symbol, also in scrambled order. Determine which alternative matches the three columns properly (your answers will read something like A-1-W or B-3-X).

	Symbol		Name		Meaning
A.	♭	1.	ledger lines	W.	lines above and below the regular staff
B.	♯	2.	natural	X.	raises the pitch of a note by one half step
C.	♮	3.	sharp	Y.	lowers the pitch of a note by one half step
D.	(ledger lines)	4.	flat	Z.	cancels the effect of previous sharps or flats

Alternatives

		part
a.	I'm not sure. Please show me.	139
b.	A-2-Y B-3-Z C-4-X C-1-W	134
ⓒ.	A-4-Y B-3-X C-2-Z D-1-W	127
d.	A-4-Y B-2-Z C-3-X D-1-W	143

Congratulations for resisting the impulse to guess. Let's pretend for a moment that the distance between the notes A and B could be measured as one-half inch:

```
    B
    ↑
    ↓
    A
```

What kind of symbol would you use if you wanted to indicate a note halfway between them? Well, you have a choice. You can use a

SHARP (♯) with the bottom note, A. THE SHARP RAISES THE PITCH OF A NOTE BY ONE HALF STEP. The new note, called A-sharp, would be halfway between A and B.

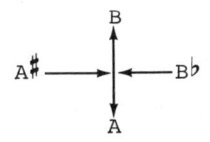

```
              B
              ↑
    A♯ ——————|—————— B♭
              ↓
              A
```

The other choice you have is to use a FLAT (♭) with the top note, B. THE FLAT LOWERS THE PITCH OF THE NOTE BY ONE HALF STEP. The new note would be called B-flat. Even though they appear different on the staff, B-flat is actually the same note as A-sharp, in that the sound of the two is the same.

The next musical symbol you saw was a natural: ♮. A NATURAL CANCELS THE EFFECT OF PREVIOUS SHARPS OR FLATS. For example, if you wanted to write three notes in a row, C, then C-sharp, and C again, you would put a natural sign in front of the last C to tell the performer to cancel the effect of the previous sharp. (See the example below.)

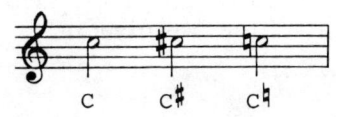

```
    C    C♯   C♮
```

The first note and the third note are the same. The natural sign would not be necessary if the middle note were removed.

In Chapter 1 you learned about staff lines. When you want to write a note that goes higher or lower than the staff, use short lines called LEDGER LINES to put the note on. Recall the use of a ledger line earlier in this chapter for the notation of middle C.

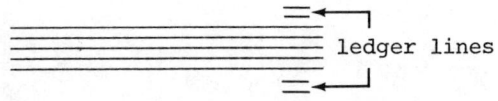

```
    ═══════════
    ─────────── ┐
    ─────────── │ ledger lines
    ─────────── ┘
    ═══════════
```

Now return to the question in part 138.

140

You made a mistake and need an explanation to clarify the problem. Go to part 125.

141

Some of the notes in this answer are right, but you did make a mistake.

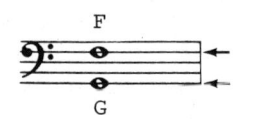

Two lines are particularly important for remembering notes in the bass clef. Do you see the two dots in the bass clef sign? Between them is the first important line. Notes on that line are always named F. The bottom line of the bass staff is always called G. From those two notes you can determine the other notes on the clef. For example, a note on the first space (right above G) would be A. As in the treble clef, the notes go from A to G and then start over with A.

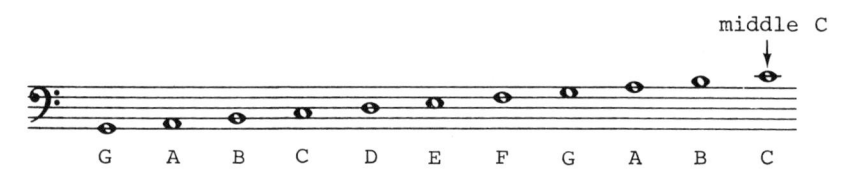

G A B C D E F G A B C

Be sure to assign a letter to every line and every space. By being careful not to skip notes, and by remembering the two key lines illustrated in the example at the top of the page, you can readily recall the notes of the bass clef.

If you would like to do a short exercise on the bass clef, turn to part 130. If you feel that the exercise is not necessary, return to part 126.

142

Diagnostic Question Six

Another term you should know is OCTAVE. Which of the measures below (1, 2, or 3) is an example of an octave?

Alternatives

		part
a.	I don't know.	145
b.	measure 1	160
c.	measure 2	147
d.	measure 3	156

143

No, you must have mixed up the answers somewhere. A brief review should help you find your error. Turn to part 134.

144

Excellent. Here's hoping you can do as well on the next question, which is similar. Go to part 154.

145

You were asked to identify an octave. Recall that the notes of the staff are named from A through G, and then they start over again with A. The distance from one A through the next A is called an octave. B through B, C through C, D through D, and so forth, are also octaves.

Which measure has the octave in this example?

In measure 1 the bottom note is D. It is one step above middle C. Counting up one note for each line and each space, the top note in measure 1 is C. D to C is not an octave.

In measure number 2 the bottom note is still D, but the top note is one step higher than before. The top note in measure 2 is D. From D to D is an octave, so measure 2 is the correct answer.

Now return to the Diagnostic Question in part 142.

146

You missed one note and should review the subject. There's a brief review for you in part 157.

147

No, it seems you need an explanation. Go to part 145.

148

You chose the proper alternative. Are you ready to go to something else? (The appropriate response is "yes.") Fine, go to part 159.

149

Diagnostic Question Seven*

A section of the piano keyboard is pictured below. Notice that the short black keys are in alternating groups of two and three.

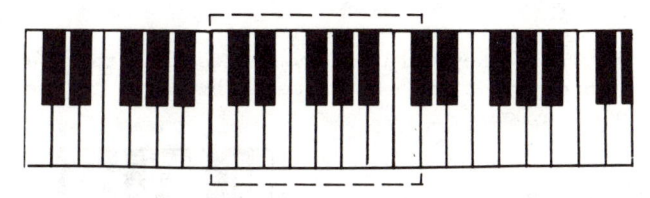

When a picture of the keyboard is used hereafter, only a small section—like the one within the dotted lines—will be shown.

Every key on the piano will sound a note, and that note can be written on the staff. The notes on the piano keyboard have the same names as notes on the staff (A, B, C, D, E, F, G, A, B, etc.), and you should learn them.

In the section of the keyboard pictured below, five keys are numbered. Can you select the correct alternative by identifying the letter name of each numbered key?

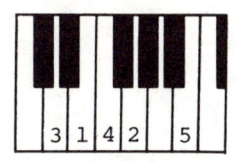

Alternatives

		part
a.	I am not familiar with the piano keyboard. Will you explain it to me?	150
b.	1 = B 3 = D 2 = A 4 = C 5 = F	173
c.	1 = E 3 = G 2 = F 4 = A 5 = D	155
(d.)	1 = E 3 = D 2 = G 4 = F 5 = B	144

*If you have already answered this question once, correctly answer it again and continue the program.

150

While learning the names of notes from A to G, you also learned the position of middle C on the staff—between the bass and treble clefs.

The first note to learn on the piano is also middle C. You might wonder how many notes are named C on the keyboard. There are quite a few—one for every octave.

In the picture of the keyboard below, notice that the black keys are arranged in groups of two or three. These groups are repeated up and down the keyboard.

The first thing you need to remember is that the notes A, B, C, D, E, F, G are the long, white keys. The black keys are for sharps or flats.

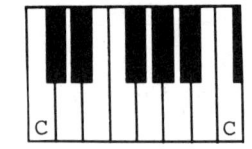

Directly to the LEFT of the two black keys is C. Find C on the picture of the keyboard. Between the two black keys and right next to C, is D. Then come E, F, G, A, and B (all white keys). Then the notes start over with C again.

For the present you should fix in your mind two particular white keys: the C directly left of the two black keys, and the F directly left of the three black keys. Find F on the keyboard.

Turn to part 152.

151

That was a good choice. Obviously, you realize that a black key between two white keys has two names.

The black key on the left can properly be called either C-sharp (because it is directly above C) or D-flat (because it is directly below D).

Now we must return to the word "octave," which you learned earlier.

The next step in the program is in part 166.

152

Use the Shield

On the piano keyboard the sharps and flats are generally found on the _____ keys.

☙

black

The notes A, B, C, D, E, F, and G are on the _____ keys.

☙

white

The black keys are in groups of two and three. Directly left of the two black keys is the note _____ .

☙

C

The arrow in this example is pointing to the note _____ .

☙

C

Does C appear on the keyboard more than one time?

☙

yes

The white key directly right of C is _____ .

☙

D

The key to the left of the three black notes is the note _____ .

☙

F

Turn to part 153.

153

Use the Shield

In this picture, number 1 is the note _____ , and number 2 is the note _____ .

❧

C, F

Here, number 1 is the note _____ , and number 2 is the note _____ .

❧

D, G

What are the names of notes 1, 2, and 3 here?

❧

E, F, A

What are the names of the numbered notes here?

❧

D, E, A

Of the numbered notes, which is A?

❧

2

Which key in that last frame is E?

❧

1

What key is number 3 in the example above?

❧

B

Now return to the Diagnostic Question in part 149.

154

Diagnostic Question Eight

Choose the alternate which properly identifies all five keys numbered to the right.

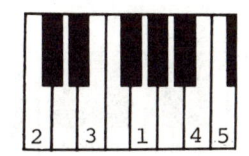

Alternatives

				part
a.	I am uncertain about this question.			150
b.	1 = G 3 = E			
	2 = C 4 = B			
	5 = C			148
c.	1 = D 3 = B			
	2 = F 4 = E			
	5 = G			157
d.	1 = G 3 = E			
	2 = F 4 = B			
	5 = C			146

(b. is circled)

155

No, that wasn't entirely correct. For an explanation of this question, go to part 150.

156

No, not quite. To understand why, go to part 145.

157

That alternative was incorrect. See if this review will refresh your memory.

There are two keys you need to recognize quickly when you look at a keyboard. The first is directly left of the two black keys (number 1). It is C. The second key is F, which is directly left of the three black keys (number 2).

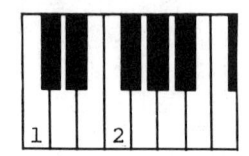

Remember also that the notes A, B, C, D, E, F, and G are the white keys. The black keys are used for sharps and flats.

By remembering the places of C and F on the keyboard, you can determine all the other notes. STUDY THE ABOVE EXAMPLE BEFORE GOING ON.

The above discussion is intended only as a short reminder. If you have not had previous experience with the piano keyboard, or if you feel that you need a longer review, turn to part 150.

If you are sure the above discussion is a sufficient reminder, return to the Diagnostic Question in part 154.

158

No, that is too small for an octave. To learn why, turn to part 176.

159

Diagnostic Question Nine

Not only do the white keys of the piano have names, but the black keys have names as well. Identify the numbered black keys in the following example to pick your alternative.

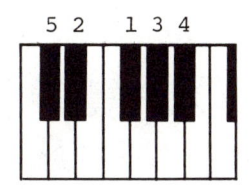

```
5 2   1 3 4
```

Alternatives

		part
a.	I think I should let you show me.	161
b.	1 = G♭ or F♯ 3 = A♭ or G♯	
	2 = D♭ or C♯ 4 = B♯ or C♭	
	5 = C♯ or D♭	163
(c.)	1 = F♯ or G♭ 3 = A♭ or G♯	
	2 = D♯ or E♭ 4 = A♯ or B♭	
	5 = D♭ or C♯	151
d.	1 = F♯ or G♭ 3 = A♯ or B♭	
	2 = E♭ or D♯ 4 = B♯ or C♭	
	5 = C♯ or D♭	164

160

Right! An octave is the distance from A to A, B to B, C to C, D to D, and so on. Measure 1 was from E to E.

Until now we have been dealing with music as it is written on the staff. Obviously, music must be played or sung to be heard. The most common musical instrument is the human voice, but many other instruments (piano, organ, and harpsichord) employ a keyboard. It is now time to become acquainted with the keyboard.

Go to part 149.

The first thing to remember about black keys is that they are used only as sharps and flats. You also need to understand that a black key can have two names.

The black key in the example on the right is between F and G. It can be called F-sharp because it is directly above F; or it can be called G-flat because it is directly below G. Both names are correct; they refer to the same note. Let's look at another example:

Black key number 1 is halfway between D and E. Therefore, the key can be called D-sharp or E-flat. Either name is correct, depending on the music in which the note is used.

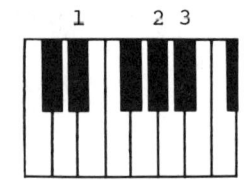

Black key number 2 is between G and A. It can, therefore, be called G-sharp or A-flat. Black key 3, between A and B, can be called A-sharp or B-flat. Thus, every black key has two possible names.

Use the Shield

This black key between C and D can be called C-sharp or _____ . Either name is correct.

❧

D-flat

This black key between F and G therefore, can be called either _____ sharp or _____ flat.

❧

F-sharp, G-flat

The two names of this black key are _____ and _____ .

❧

A-sharp, B-flat

Continue in part 162.

162

Use the Shield

Which black key is D-flat?

❧

number 1

Another name for the key we call D-flat is _____ .

❧

C-sharp

The two names for the key under number 3 are _____ and _____ .

❧

F-sharp, G-flat

A-sharp (B-flat) is found under number _____ .

❧

5

Number 4 is G-sharp or _____ .

❧

A-flat

Now carefully choose the correct answer to the Diagnostic Question in part 159.

163

The black keys are causing you some confusion. Read carefully the brief explanation in part 161.

Some of the notes you identified were incorrect.

Here are four points for you to remember:

1. The black keys are used for sharps and flats only.

2. Every black key has two names, one using a sharp ($\sharp$), and the other using a flat ($\flat$).

3. Every black key is between two white keys. For example, this one is between C and D:

4. The black key is named by putting a sharp with the name of the lower white key (here, C-sharp), or by putting a flat with the name of the higher white key (here, D-flat). Both C-sharp and D-flat are correct names for this black key.

The same is true with any black key. If you find the names of the two white keys on either side, and PUT A SHARP WITH THE LOWER ONE, OR A FLAT WITH THE HIGHER ONE, you will have the black-key name.

This was only a short review. If the concept of black keys still seems at all strange to you, turn to part 161.

If this review is sufficient, return to the Diagnostic Question in part 159 and see if you can answer it correctly.

No, you are mistaken, but the mistake is easy to correct.

If you start at the left of the keyboard and play every note (that is, every white and black key) from left to right, you are playing HALF STEPS. A half step is the smallest step on the piano keyboard. EVERY NOTE IS ONE HALF STEP FROM ITS CLOSEST NEIGHBOR.

Even if two white keys do not have a black key between them the two keys are still a half step apart. (See the example.)

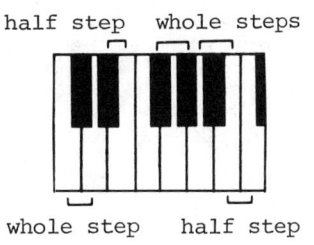

Notice, however, that if there is a key between the two given keys, they are a whole step apart.

Return to the Diagnostic Question in part 170.

166

Diagnostic Question Ten

At the base of the keyboard below are three numbered arrows. One of them covers exactly an octave on the keyboard; the other two do not. Which arrow points out an octave?

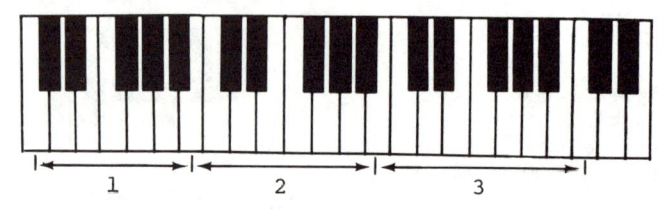

Alternatives

		part
a.	I'm not sure which arrow points out an octave. Please explain.	176
b.	Arrow 1	158
c.	Arrow 2	188
d.	Arrow 3	171

167

Right. If there is no black key between two white keys, the white keys are a half step apart. If there is a black key between them, the white keys are a whole step apart. Now go to part 174.

168

The problem is to find the white keys on a piano keyboard that are only one half step apart. Do you recall the statement made earlier that every key is only one half step from its nearest neighboring key, black or white?

Look at the note C in the example. The nearest key to the right of C is the black key C-sharp. Therefore, the distance from C to C-sharp is one half step. From the black key C-sharp to its nearest neighbor (D) is also one half step. Thus, there are two half steps from C to D—or one whole step.

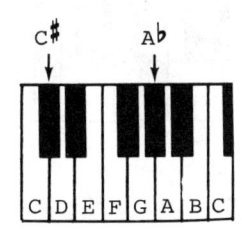

```
        C#      Ab
        ↓       ↓
    ┌─┬─┬─┬─┬─┬─┬─┐
    │ │█│ │█│ │█│█│
    │ │█│ │█│ │█│█│
    │ └┬┘ └┬┘ └┬┘ │
    │C │D│E│F│G│A│B│C│
    └──┴─┴─┴─┴─┴─┴──┘
```

We can conclude the following: If there is one key between any two given keys, the two given keys are ONE WHOLE STEP apart. If there is no key between them, the keys are one half step apart. For example, from C to D is a whole step because there is a black key between them. G to A-flat is a half step because there is no note between them.

When you are asked to show which white keys are only one half step apart, the white keys WITHOUT BLACK KEYS BETWEEN THEM are the ones you must find. Keep that in mind as you complete the following exercises.

Continue in part 177.

169

You've overlooked an important point. To discover it go to part 168.

170

Diagnostic Question Eleven

In the next example, the brackets show the two locations on the keyboard where there are no black keys between the white keys.

If there is NO black key between two white keys, the white keys are said to be:

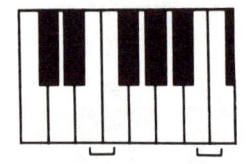

Alternatives

		part
a.	one half step apart	167
b.	one whole step apart	165

(a is circled)

171

Well, you've made an error. You should read the explanation on keyboard octaves. Go to part 176.

172

Correct. The half steps must fall between steps 3 to 4 and 7 to 8 of the major scale. In the scale of G-major (GABCDEF#G), the half steps must fall between B to C and F to G. Because F to G is a whole step (there is a black key between them), the step must be made smaller. This is done by raising the F to F-sharp. The resulting step (F-sharp to G) is the desired half step. The scale of G-major will therefore always have F-sharp in it. Try applying the major scale pattern to another key in part 186.

173

You were mistaken in your choice. Please read on.

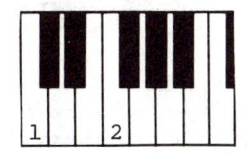

There are two keys that can serve as guideposts for all keys. The first one is directly left of the two black keys (number 1 in the example above). That key is C. The second guidepost is F; it is directly left of the three black keys (number 2). Remember also that all the white keys are used for the notes A, B, C, D, E, F, and G. The black keys are used for sharps and flats.
By recalling the positions of C and F on the keyboard, you can determine all the other notes. STUDY THE ABOVE EXAMPLE AND LEARN TO IDENTIFY THE POSITION OF EACH NOTE BEFORE GOING ON.

The preceding discussion is intended only as a short reminder. If you have not had previous experience with the piano keyboard go to part 150 for a thorough review.

If you think the reminder has been sufficient, return to the Diagnostic Question in part 149.

174

Diagnostic Question Twelve

Which white keys in this example are only one half step from each other?

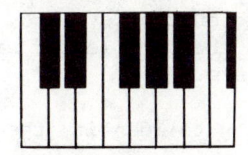

Alternatives

		part
a.	I believe you should explain it.	168
b.	E to F only	178
c.	E to F and B to C	189
d.	C to D and F to G	169

175

You are right. The half steps in the key of F-major fall between A and B-flat, and E and F. The key of F-major will, therefore, always have a B-flat.

As you have seen, certain keys always need to use flats or sharps to conform to the half-step spacing between steps 3 to 4 and 7 to 8 of their scales. Do you know how these sharps and flats are indicated on a music score? More on this subject in part 190.

176

When we first used the term OCTAVE, we were talking about the music staff. If you start with A on the staff and proceed through G, you must continue to A to complete the octave. It is exactly the same on the piano keyboard. An octave is the distance from A to A, B to B, C to C, and so forth, whether on the staff or on the keyboard.

When asked to find an octave on the keyboard, you first need to name the starting key. Then, count up the musical alphabet until you arrive at the same letter name you started with. In so doing, you will cover an octave.

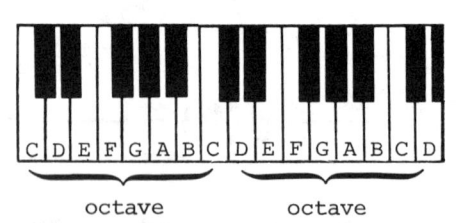

Two octaves are marked in the above example (C to C, and D to D). There are many other octaves shown as well: E to E, F to F, A to A, etc.

Briefly, to find an octave on the keyboard, identify any key and find the nearest key with the same letter name. An octave is located between these two keys.

Now you should find it easy to identify the octave in part 166.

177

Use the Shield

On the piano keyboard the distance from C to D is a _____ step.

❧

whole (There is a black key between them.)

From B to C is a _____ step.

❧

half (no key between)

From G to A-flat is a _____ step.

❧

half

From F-sharp to G-sharp is a _____ step.

❧

whole (The key G is between)

From E to F-sharp is a _____ step.

❧

whole (F is between)

Now return to the Diagnostic Question in part 174.

178

Your answer was partially right but you need a brief explanation. You will find it in part 168.

Diagnostic Question Thirteen

C-major scale

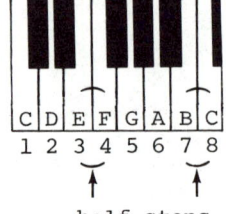

A SCALE is a series of notes within any octave (e.g., C to C or D to D) that follows a particular arrangement of whole and half steps. The effect of the arrangement is to give one tone dominance over the others so that they seem to be "pulled" toward it. If you count the first note in the octave as number 1 and give the rest of the notes—in order of ascending pitch—the numbers 2 to 8, major scales will have half steps between steps 3 to 4 and 7 to 8. (See the example above.) All other steps are whole steps.

To summarize, a major scale consists of eight notes within an octave arranged in a set pattern of whole steps and half steps. The half steps lie between steps 3 to 4 and 7 to 8.

Let's see if you can apply this rule to another major scale. In the scale of G-major (beginning and ending on G), the half steps will fall between which notes?

G-major scale

Alternatives

		part
a.	I'm not sure. Please explain further.	180
b.	B-sharp to C and F-sharp to G	195
c.	B to C and F to G	187
d.	B to C and F-sharp to G	172

All right, let's take a more detailed look at the major scale.

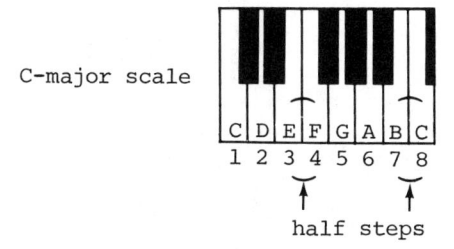

C-major scale

[Keyboard diagram showing C D E F G A B C, numbered 1-8, with half steps marked between 3-4 (E-F) and 7-8 (B-C)]

half steps

We are using the C-major scale to observe where the half steps fall in a major scale because it shows the half steps without using black keys. All other major scales use some black keys to get the half steps in the right places. Remember: ALL MAJOR SCALES HAVE HALF STEPS BETWEEN NOTES 3 to 4 AND 7 to 8 OF THE ASCENDING SCALE.

You can form a major scale in any octave by numbering the notes 1 through 8, as we did above, and putting half steps in the designated places, making sure all other steps are whole steps. For example:

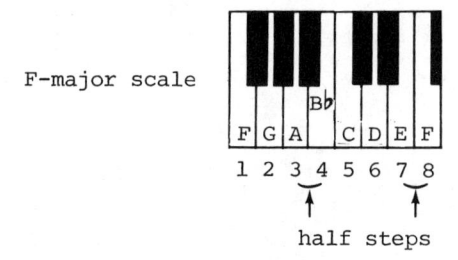

F-major scale

[Keyboard diagram showing F G A Bb C D E F, numbered 1-8, with half steps marked between 3-4 and 7-8]

half steps

B♭ is needed here to create the half step from 3 to 4. (A half step already exists between E and F.)

Here is another example:

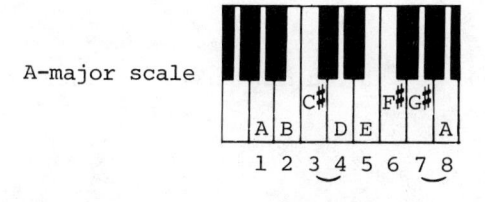

A-major scale

[Keyboard diagram showing A B C# D E F# G# A, numbered 1-8, with half steps marked between 3-4 and 7-8]

Sharps are needed here to create the major-scale pattern of whole steps and half steps.

Go to part 181.

181

Use the Shield

If you number the notes in this scale, the lower G will be note number 1 and B will be note number _____ .

∽

3

Every step in the major scale is a whole step except the steps 3-4 and _____ .

∽

7-8

The steps 3-4 and 7-8 are (*whole/half*) steps.

∽

half

Steps 3 and 4 in the G-major scale fall on notes _____ and _____ .

∽

B, C

Steps 7 and 8 fall on notes _____ and _____ in the G-major scale.

∽

F♯ , G

In a G-major scale, there are no keys between B and C, or between _____ and _____ .

∽

F♯ , G

Now return to part 179 and see if you can answer the Diagnostic Question correctly.

182

You have mixed up two of the key signatures. Go on to part 192.

183

You have chosen the wrong alternative. Please read the explanation in part 184.

184

All right, let's examine the key of F-major step by step.

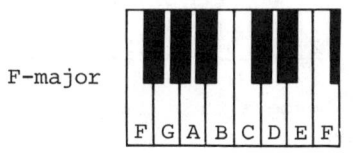

F-major

First, number the notes from 1 to 8, beginning with the first note of the scale. For F-major, begin on F, just as for G-major you began on G. Note number 8, the last one, should have the same letter name as note number 1.

```
F G A B C D E F
1 2 3 4 5 6 7 8
```

Since you are looking for steps 3 to 4 and 7 to 8, you now look for the notes which have the appropriate numbers. Steps 3 and 4 are A and B; 7 and 8 are E and F.

The next step is to make sure that steps 3 to 4 and 7 to 8 are half steps—that there are no keys between them. Since step 3 to 4 is A to B, there is a black key between them. An adjustment is needed. If you substitute B-flat for B, the step becomes a half step and the problem is solved. F-major will, therefore, always use B-flat instead of B for its fourth step. Step 7 to 8 is E to F—a half step as it stands—so no adjustment is needed there.

Return now to answer the Diagnostic Question in part 186.

185

That alternative was incorrect. A brief review should clear up your problem. Go to part 192.

186

Diagnostic Question Fourteen

Now see if you can find steps 3 to 4 and 7 to 8 in the key of F-major.

F-major scale [keyboard diagram: F G A B C D E F]

When you have found them, choose the alternative below that correctly lists the half steps:

Alternatives

		part
a.	I'm still unsure.	184
b.	A to B-flat and E to F	175
c.	B to C and E to F	191
d.	B-flat to C and F-sharp to G	183

187

Not quite. You forgot one important detail. To brush up on this subject turn to part 180.

188

That is correct. An octave is the distance from A to A, B to B, C to C, and so forth, whether on the staff or keyboard. For your next step go to part 170.

189

Congratulations. You remembered that the distance from one key to its nearest neighbor is always a half step. Therefore, the half steps are between E and F, and B and C. By learning the location of half steps, you have mastered one of the prime factors governing major scales. For more on this subject, go to part 179.

Diagnostic Question Fifteen

Rather than continually writing and rewriting the sharps or flats before the notes that require them in a particular key, musicians long ago devised a system of grouping the sharps and flats next to the meter signature. Such a group is called the KEY SIGNATURE. Several signatures are shown below.

A key signature may be defined as a group of sharps or flats appearing at the beginning of each staff of music to indicate the key of the music. Key signatures show the performer what notes in the scale must be altered so that all steps of the scale are whole steps except steps 3 to 4 and 7 to 8, which are half steps. Just as a meter signature establishes the beat, key signatures establish the key of the music. Match the examples on the left with the proper key on the right.

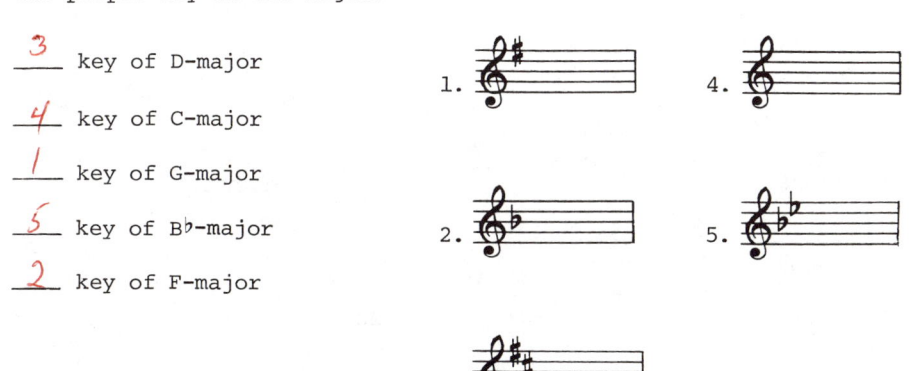

_3_ key of D-major

_4_ key of C-major

_1_ key of G-major

_5_ key of B♭-major

_2_ key of F-major

Alternatives

		part
a.	I need an explanation before attempting to answer this question.	192
b.	1 = key of G-major 4 = key of C-major 2 = key of F-major 5 = key of B♭-major 3 = key of D-major	194
c.	1 = key of F-major 4 = key of G-major 2 = key of B♭-major 5 = key of C-major 3 = key of D-major	182
d.	1 = key of C-major 4 = key of B♭-major 2 = key of F-major 5 = key of D-major 3 = key of G-major	185

(b. is circled)

191

No, you have chosen the wrong answer. Please read part 184.

192

O.K., read the following carefully. Earlier you learned that the key of G-major would always need an F-sharp to provide the half step between 7 and 8. The key signature for G-major, therefore, is F-sharp, as shown on the right.

We determined that F-major would always need a B-flat to locate the half step between 3 and 4 properly. F-major will, therefore, always use B-flat for its key signature.

We know that C-major has no sharps or flats; therefore, the key signature for C-major has no sharps or flats.

Two keys we have not discussed are B♭-major (two flats) and D-major (two sharps). Both are shown on the right.

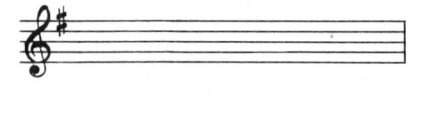

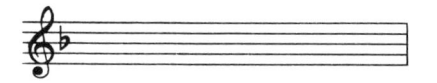

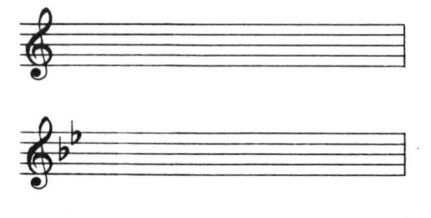

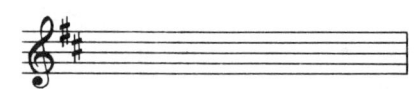

These five key signatures are the ones most commonly used in beginning music. You probably know the signatures for the first three, and need to memorize only the last two. Although many teachers devise "crutches" to help students learn the signatures, they must eventually be memorized anyway, so energy and time can be saved by doing it right away.

Turn to part 193.

193

Use the Shield

What are the five key signatures we need to memorize?

☙

C-, D-, F-, G-, and B♭-major

Which one has no sharps or flats?

☙

C-major

The key of G-major needs how many sharps or flats?

☙

1 sharp, F♯

The key of D-major needs how many sharps or flats?

☙

2 sharps, F♯ and C♯

Which key needs two flats?

☙

B♭-major; it needs B♭ and E♭

Which key needs one flat?

☙

F-major; it needs B♭

Put the Shield Aside

Now write the number of sharps or flats needed in each of the following key signatures.

C-major =   F-major =   G-major =
                     B♭-major =   D-major =

Please return to part 190 and see if you can answer the Diagnostic Question.

194

Congratulations! You have now reached the end of chapter 3. Although you don't need to memorize them now, take a minute to look at all the major key signatures. They are found in the Appendix, part 415. Then proceed with the Proficiency Developers in part 196.

195

Did you misunderstand the question? In any event you need to give some more thought to the formation of a major scale. Go to part 180.

196

Proficiency Developers

It is important that you actually DO these activities, not just read them. Please do not neglect this important part of your learning.

1. Look at the song, "There Was a Woman, Old and Gray" (part 197) and identify every note in the song by name.

2. Find a piano, organ, set of bells, xylophone, or any other keyboard instrument and count the number of notes named "C" on it. Then do the same thing for several other notes as well. Are there the same number of notes bearing each name, or does the number vary?

Please turn to part 199.

197

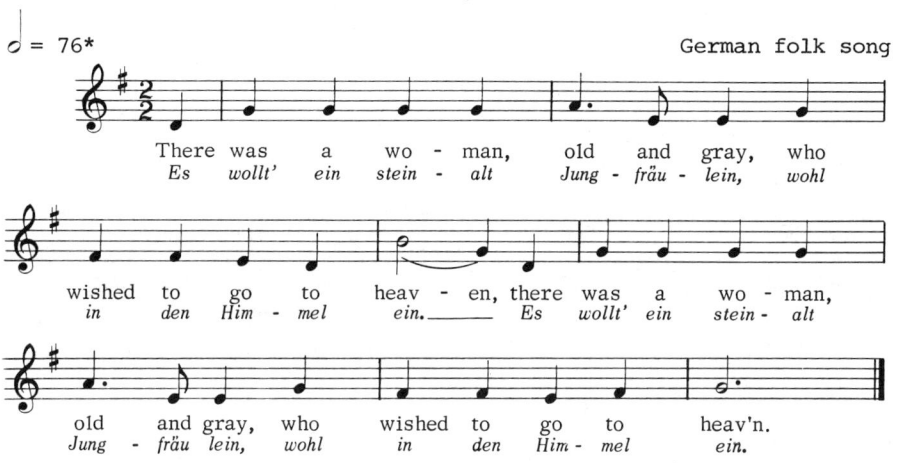

THERE WAS A WOMAN, OLD AND GRAY

♩ = 76*

German folk song

There was a wo-man, old and gray, who wished to go to heav-en, there was a wo-man, old and gray, who wished to go to heav'n.

Es wollt' ein stein-alt Jung-fräu-lein, wohl in den Him-mel ein. Es wollt' ein stein-alt Jung-fräu-lein, wohl in den Him-mel ein.

English

But there stood Peter by the gate,
And would not let her enter,
But there stood Peter by the gate,
And would not let her in.

Oh why, oh why will you not let
Me into heaven's glory?
Oh why, oh why will you not let
Me past the heavenly gate?

Because while you were down on earth,
You never kissed a man,
Because while you were down on earth,
You never kissed a man.

But then the woman, old and gray,
Kissed Peter on the cheek!
But then the woman, old and gray,
Kissed Peter on the cheek!

German

*Da stand der Petrus vor dem Tor
Und liess es nicht hinein.
Da stand der Petrus vor dem Tor
Und liess es nicht hinein.*

*Warum, warum lässt du mich nicht
Wohl in den Himmel ein?
Warum, warum lässt du mich nicht
Wohl in den Himmel ein?*

*Weil du auf dieser ganzen Welt
Noch keinen Mann geküsst.
Weil du auf dieser ganzen Welt
Noch keinen Mann geküsst.*

*Da fiel das stein alt Jungfräulein
Den Petrus um den Hals!
Da fiel das stein alt Jungfräulein
Dem Petrus um den Hals!*

Continued on part 198.

*The tempo of the music should be 76 half notes per minute.

Then laughed the angels up above, Ha-ha, ha-ha, ha-ha,... Then laughed the angels up above, Ha-ha, ha-ha, ha-ha!	*Da lachten alle Engellein,* *Ha-ha, ha-ha, ha-ha,* *Da lachten alle Engellein,* *Ha-ha, ha-ha, ha-ha!*
Then laughed the devils down below, Hi-hi, hi-hi, hi-hi! Then laughed the devils down below, Hi-hi, hi-hi, hi-hi!	*Da lachten alle Teufellein,* *Hi-hi, hi-hi, hi-hi,* *Da lachten alle Teufellein,* *Hi - hi, hi - hi, hi - hi!*
And then laughed Peter merrily, Ho-ho, ho-ho, ho-ho, And then laughed Peter merrily, Ho-ho, ho-ho, ho-ho!	*Da lachte selbst der Petrus,* *Ho-ho, ho-ho, ho-ho,* *Da lachte selbst der Petrus,* *Ho-ho, ho-ho, ho-ho!*
And so the heavens did rejoice, And open up the gates,... And so the heavens did rejoice, And open up the gates.	*Da lacht' das ganze Himmelreich,* *Ha-ha, hi-hi, ho-ho,* *Da lacht' das ganze Himmelreich,* *Ha-ha, hi-hi, ho-ho!*

3. While sitting in front of a keyboard, close your eyes and touch one of the notes. Open your eyes and identify it. Repeat the process until you can name the notes rapidly.

4. Practice saying the names of the notes in "Alouette." Then say the names of the notes in the correct rhythm. Practice playing the melody on some musical instrument.

ALOUETTE

French Canadian Folk Song

A - lou - et - te, gen - tille A - lou - et - te,
A - lou - et - te, je te plu - me - rai   Je te plu - me - rai la tête,
je te plu - me - rai la tête. Et la tête, et la tête. Oh! _____   *D.C. al Fine*

    2. Je te plumerai le bec
    3. Je te plumerai le nez
    4. Je te plumerai le dos
    5. Je te plumerai le cou

Please go to part 200.

5. Practice playing the top line of "Billy Boy" with your right hand on the piano keyboard. After rehearsing your left hand alone as well, practice playing the entire piece with both hands. If no piano is available, use another instrument that has a keyboard, playing either hand, or both hands if possible.

200

BILLY BOY

1. Oh, where have you been Bil-ly Boy, Bil-ly Boy? Oh, where have you been char-ming Bil-ly? I have been to take a wife, She's the joy of my life. She's a young thing and can-not leave her moth-er.

2. Did she ask you to come in, Billy Boy, Billy Boy?
   Did she ask you to come in, charmin' Billy?
   She did ask me to come in, with a dimple in her chin,
   She's a young thing and cannot leave her mother.

3. Did she ask you to sit down, Billy Boy, Billy Boy?
   Did she ask you to sit down, charmin' Billy?
   Yes she asked me to sit down, with a curtsey to the ground,
   She's a young thing and cannot leave her mother.

4. Did she set for you a chair, Billy Boy, Billy Boy?
   Did she set for you a chair, charmin' Billy?
   Yes she set for me a chair, she has ringlets in her hair,
   She's a young thing and cannot leave her mother.

Continued on the following page.

5. How old is she, Billy Boy, Billy Boy?
   How old is she, charmin' Billy?
   Three times six, four times seven, twenty eight and eleven,
   She's a young thing and cannot leave her mother.

6. How tall is she, Billy Boy, Billy Boy?
   How tall is she charmin' Billy?
   She's as tall as any pine, and as straight as a pumpkin vine.
   She's a young thing and cannot leave her mother.

7. Can she make a cherry pie, Billy Boy, Billy Boy?
   Can she make a cherry pie, charmin' Billy?
   She can make a cherry pie quick as a cat can wink her eye,
   She's a young thing and cannot leave her mother.

8. Does she often go to church, Billy Boy, Billy Boy?
   Does she often go to church, charmin' Billy?
   Yes she often goes to church, with her bonnet white as birch,
   She's a young thing and cannot leave her mother.

9. Can she make a pudding well, Billy Boy, Billy Boy?
   Can she make a pudding well, charmin' Billy?
   She can make a pudding well, I can tell it by the smell,
   She's a young thing and cannot leave her mother.

Go to part 201.

201

6. Copy the following clef signs and key signatures on the blank staves below:

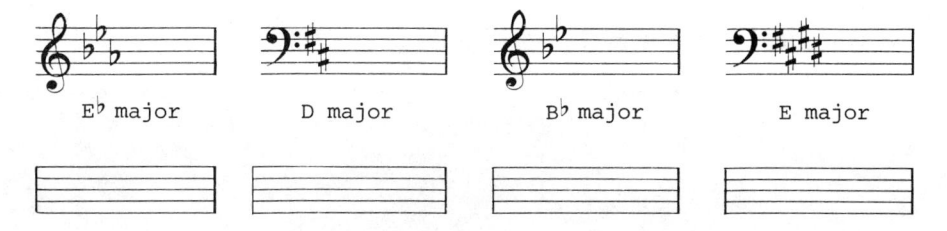

   E♭ major   D major   B♭ major   E major

« Just for Fun »

Before you take the Self-Test, turn to part 202 and solve the *Secret Code*.

202

SECRET CODE*

Can you solve the secret messages written below by filling in letters where the notes are? (Be sure to notice the clef designation at the left of the staff!)

1.

[Treble clef staff with notes and letters: M _ T _ M _ _ Y TH _ OL _ O _ K _ T]

[Treble clef staff with notes and letters: MI _ NI _ HT # _ OR TH _ MI _ RO _ ILM - _ OR _]

2.

[Bass clef staff with notes and letters: _ _ _ _ WILL _ R _ Y TO _ T]

[Bass clef staff with notes and letters: YOU _ N _ TH _ OL _ TOWN _ RI _ _ _ L]

3. Now try this one . . . ask your teacher what this sign means:

[Alto clef staff with notes and letters: _ N _ YOU _ R _ _ _ _ - _ L _ ?]

(Each message is decoded in part 414.)

Turn to part 203 for the Self-Test. By taking the test and grading your results, you can determine what parts of the chapter need review.

*Used with permission, Karen Kammerer, University of Oregon, Eugene, Oregon.

Self-Test

Match the musical terms and symbols on the left side of the page with their proper definitions from the list on the right.

1. pitch __F__
2. octave __D__
3. key signature __A__
4. sharp __B__
5. flat __G__
6. natural __E__
7. major scale __C__

A. a group of sharps or flats placed at the beginning of the staff to identify the key.

B. raises the pitch of a note by one half step.

C. comprised of whole steps except for steps 3 to 4 and 7 to 8, which are half steps.

D. the distance from A to A, B to B, etc.

E. cancels previous sharps or flats.

F. the highness or lowness of a note.

G. lowers the pitch of a note by only one half step.

8. How many sharps or flats are in the key signature for D-major? __2 #'s__

9. How many sharps or flats are in the key signature for F-major? __1 b__

10. How many sharps or flats are in the key signature for B♭-major? __2 b's__

11. Write the following notes on the treble staff shown below: B, F♯, D, G, F, A, E♭, middle C.

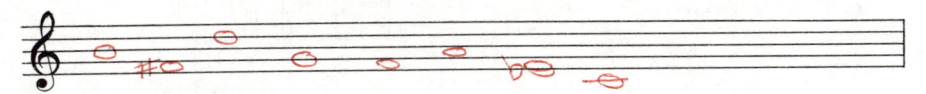

12. Write these notes on the bass staff shown below: F, G, B♭, A, C, D♯, E.

Continued in part 204.

13. In the following space, write the names of all the notes in the melody (treble staff only) of "Billy Boy" (part 200).

   line 1:
   line 2:
   line 3:

Identify each numbered key in the examples below by writing its name in the appropriate blank.

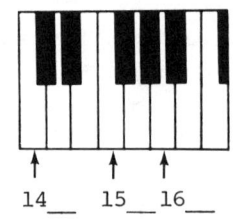

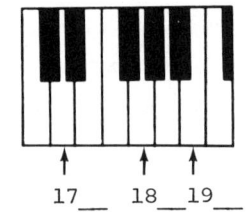

14__ 15__ 16__

17__ 18__ 19__

Match the numbered black keys with the appropriate letters from the right.

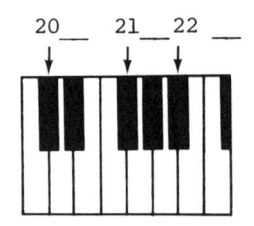

20__ 21__ 22__

L. F-sharp or G-flat

M. C-sharp or D-flat

N. A-sharp or B-flat

Using 1/1 for whole and 1/2 for half, write the fraction that properly describes the intervals shown on this keyboard.

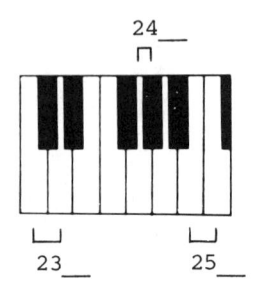

24__

23__   25__

End of test

After completing the test, turn to part 205.

YOU HAVE NOW COMPLETED THE SELF-TEST. Check your answers with the key that follows and grade your results. If you missed a substantial number of the items you probably need to read the chapter again before going on. In any case, be sure to review each of the questions you missed by looking up the material specified in parentheses next to the answer.

Answers & Review Index

1. F (pitch defined 114)
2. D (octave defined 145, 176)
3. A (key signature defined 190)
4. B (sharps 139)
5. G (flats 139)
6. E (naturals 139)
7. C (major scale 180 ff)
8. two sharps (key signatures 192)
9. one flat (key signatures 192)
10. two flats (key signatures 192)

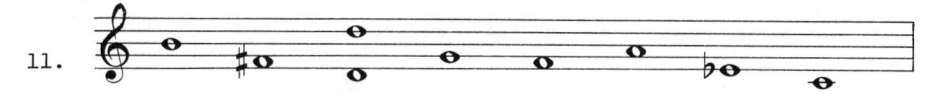

11. (notes in the treble clef 116 ff)

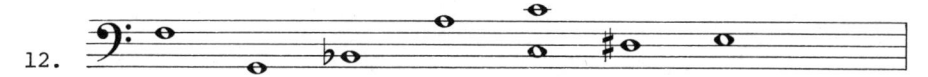

12. (notes in the bass clef 128 ff)

Answers and Review Index are continued in part 206.

13. line 1: F♯ G A A A D F♯ G A A B A F♯ G
    line 2: A A A D F♯ F♯ F♯ E E F♯
    line 3: G G G G A G F♯ E F♯ G A D B
    line 4: A F♯ A A G E C♯ E D
14. C (piano keyboard, white keys 150 ff)
15. F (piano keyboard, white keys 150 ff)
16. A (piano keyboard, white keys 150 ff)
17. D (piano keyboard, white keys 150 ff)
18. G (piano keyboard, white keys 150 ff)
19. B (piano keyboard, white keys 150 ff)
20. M (piano keyboard, black keys 161 ff)
21. L (piano keyboard, black keys 161 ff)
22. N (piano keyboard, black keys 161 ff)
23. 1/1 (piano keyboard intervals 168 ff)
24. 1/2 (piano keyboard intervals 168 ff)
25. 1/2 (piano keyboard intervals 168 ff)

4
Harmonic Structure of Music

207

In previous chapters, the basic aspects of rhythm and melody were presented. Let us now turn our attention to the third major component of music, HARMONY. Despite differences between pieces of music, close examination of tone combinations reveals some common and often repeated patterns. In this chapter you will become acquainted with several such patterns. There are nine Diagnostic Questions in this chapter.

Objectives

At the end of the chapter, you will be expected to do the following:

1. Recall definitions for the terms harmony, chord, and interval.
2. Identify the basic intervals—second, third, fourth, fifth, sixth, and seventh.
3. Recall which intervals are major or minor, perfect or imperfect.
4. Identify major and minor thirds.
5. Invert any interval or chord.
6. Recognize the definition of a triad and the differences between major and minor triads.
7. Determine whether a triad is major or minor.
8. Construct a triad on any given note.
9. Recognize which triads are primary (major) and which are secondary (minor) in any major key.
10. Recognize the I, IV, and V chords in the keys of D, B-flat, and E-major.

Go to part 208.

208

Diagnostic Question One

Professional musicians frequently find it difficult to agree on an all-inclusive definition of HARMONY because of its complexity. Simply stated, harmony is the simultaneous sounding of two or more different tones. The combination of notes sounded together is referred to as a CHORD. When persons sing together they are harmonizing, or making chords.

Which of the following statements is concerned with harmony?

Alternatives

		part
a.	The beat in that piece of music is really unusual. *rhythm*	215
b.	Have you ever heard anyone who could sing so high? *pitch*	221
c.	They were out of tune at first, but now they sound good together. *harmony*	214

209

Because you made a mistake, please read the following explanation carefully. A harmonic interval is the difference in pitch between two notes that are played together. If you played the note D and the note B together, the B would be written directly above the D like this:

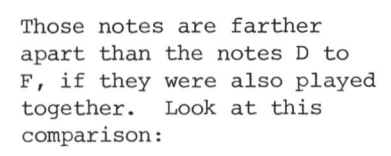

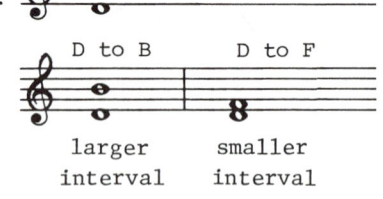

Those notes are farther apart than the notes D to F, if they were also played together. Look at this comparison:

D to B — larger interval

D to F — smaller interval

Now return to the Diagnostic Question in part 213 and see if you can answer it correctly.

210

Correct. The farther apart notes are, the larger the interval between them.

<u>Intervals are identified by numbers.</u> The identifying number for each interval is the number of SCALE TONES included in it.

For example, in the interval C to E, there are three lines and spaces—C, D, and E—so the interval is called a THIRD. This information should help you answer the next Diagnostic Question, in part 217.

211

You must have overlooked something. For an explanation, turn to part 225.

212

No, that wasn't quite right. Let's examine the problem in part 219.

Diagnostic Question Two

Another term you need to recognize is INTERVAL. An interval is the difference in pitch between two tones. A HARMONIC INTERVAL exists between two tones played simultaneously. In the example below, the intervals C to G and C to B are harmonic intervals. Because the distance between C to G is different than between C to B, they are different intervals. In this example, the harmonic interval between C to G is smaller than between C to B:

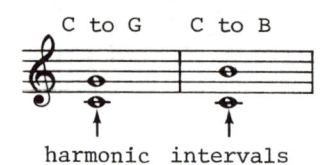

harmonic intervals

You should learn the difference between HARMONIC intervals and MELODIC intervals. Remember that a harmonic interval exists between notes that are sounded together, as illustrated in the example above. A melodic interval exists between any note and the note that immediately follows it, as illustrated below.

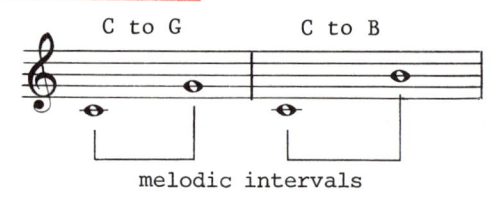

melodic intervals

Now, from the alternatives below choose the smallest and the largest intervals.

Alternatives

	smallest		largest	part
a.	1	and	4	209
b.	3	and	6	210
c.	3	and	4	220

214

Of course. If persons are singing together (simultaneously but not in unison) they are singing harmony, even if it might be dissonant harmony. Turn to part 213.

215

No, that can't be right. Why? The statement you selected mentions the beat, or the pulse, of a musical selection. Beat and pulse have to do with the rhythm of music, not its harmony. Harmony is the sounding of two or more notes together, whether it involves two persons singing together or two notes played simultaneously on an instrument. Now choose the correct response in part 208.

216

The answer you selected was incorrect. Let's see why. Turn to part 227.

217

Diagnostic Question Three

Choose the alternative below that correctly identifies the intervals of a SECOND, FIFTH, and SIXTH in that order.

Alternatives

							part
a.	I'm not sure. Where is the discussion on this matter?						219
	second		fifth		sixth		
b.	4	and	7	and	1		222
c.	6	and	1	and	3		212
d.	6	and	2	and	1		231

218

Very good. Thirds and sixths can be either major or minor; fourths and fifths are perfect, diminished, or augmented. If you decrease the size of a fourth or fifth by one half step (i.e., diminish it), it is called simply a DIMINISHED fourth or fifth. If you expand its size one half step (i.e., augment it), it is called an AUGMENTED fourth or fifth. Infrequently, other intervals also use the terms diminished and augmented, but because the terms apply to musical practices not directly related to the purpose of your study, they will not be pursued.

Up to now we have been measuring intervals according to the lines and spaces they encompass on the staff. Musicians find this process laborious, and commit the intervals to memory instead. In the same way you know that 9 times 6 equals 54, the musician knows that the interval from D up to G is a fourth. If sharps or flats are then added, it is easy to determine whether the interval is augmented or diminished. For more about measuring intervals go to part 226.

While examining the problem, remember that an interval is the distance between two notes played together or consecutively. Using the note D as a basis, here are some examples:

The bottom note is D, and the top note is E. The interval D to E encompasses only two lines and spaces and is, therefore, called a SECOND.

This harmonic interval has two notes: D and F. There is a line between them, namely E. This interval encompasses THREE lines and spaces, D, E, and F. It is a THIRD.

This melodic interval encompasses D (the bottom note), E, F, and G (the top note). Because it encompasses four lines and spaces, it is a FOURTH.

This interval is in the bass clef. The bottom note is D. The interval encompasses D, E, F, G, and A; five lines and spaces. The interval is a FIFTH.

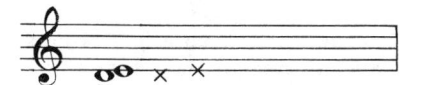

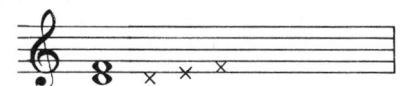

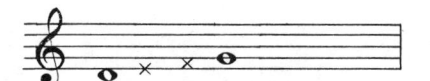

By counting an interval's bottom note and top note plus all the lines and spaces between them, you can determine the size of the interval.

Use the Shield

What is the interval's size?

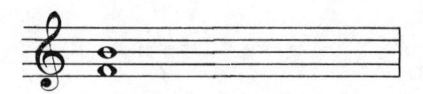

❧

It is a fourth. It encompasses F, G, A, and B—four lines and spaces.

What is the size of this interval.

❧

It is a seventh. It encompasses seven lines and spaces: F, G, A, B, C, D, and E. Please continue on the following page.

Identify the size of this
interval.

*It is a sixth. It covers all the lines and spaces between
B and G (six).*

Please return to the Diagnostic Question in part 217 and see if
you can answer it correctly.

220

You are right about the smallest interval but wrong on the largest. Go to part 209.

221

No, that can't be right. A remark about a person's ability to sing high notes is a comment on the RANGE of his voice and has nothing to do with harmony. It takes two people or two instruments, singing or playing together, to make harmony. Now choose the correct response in part 208.

222

Not quite right. For an explanation, turn to part 219.

223

Diagnostic Question Four

Here we will be concerned with two kinds of intervals only: (1) those that are usually either major or minor and (2) those that are usually either perfect, diminished, or augmented.

Do not guess on the next question. It is important that you fully understand this concept.

Which alternative correctly describes the intervals in the following example?

Alternatives

		part
a.	I would prefer an explanation before I select my response.	225
b.	Intervals 1 and 4 are usually major or minor. Intervals 2 and 3 are usually perfect, diminished, or augmented.	218
c.	Intervals 1 and 3 are usually major or minor. Intervals 2 and 4 are usually perfect, diminished, or augmented.	211

224

No, you must have made a mistake of some kind. For an explanation go to part 234.

225

third   fourth   fifth   sixth

The example above includes a third, a fourth, a fifth, and a sixth. Fourths and fifths are designated PERFECT. By adding sharps or flats, you may augment or diminish perfect intervals. If a perfect interval is increased by one half step, it is said to be AUGMENTED. When it is made one half step smaller, it is termed DIMINISHED. Hence, fourths and fifths may be perfect, augmented, or diminished.

Thirds and sixths are usually either major or minor (a minor interval is one half step smaller than a major). They cannot be referred to as perfect, although they may rarely be augmented or diminished.

QUESTION: Of the following intervals, which ones can be perfect: second, third, fourth, fifth, sixth, seventh?

ANSWER: Only fourths and fifths can be perfect.

Now return to part 223.

Diagnostic Question Five

In answering the next question and others that follow, do not guess. If you are unsure of the answer, or the process by which the answer is determined, select the first alternative and read the explanation.

Which of the following thirds are CORRECTLY labeled?

    A   B   C   D   E
  major minor major major major

Alternatives

		part
a.	I would like to read the background material before I make my choice.	227
b.	Thirds C and E are correctly labeled.	230
c.	Thirds A and D are correctly labeled.	236
d.	Thirds B and C are correctly labeled.	216

HOW TO DISTINGUISH BETWEEN MAJOR AND MINOR THIRDS

The interval of a third is the basis of traditional Western harmony. Remember, thirds can be designated major or minor, with the major third being one half step larger than the minor third. The terms MAJOR and MINOR define the QUALITY of an interval. (Its SIZE is the numerical designation, second, third, fourth, and so on.) Determining the quality of an interval involves a high-level thought process that takes some effort at first, but with time becomes as easy as multiplication tables.

Here is a three-step process for determining the quality of a third. Let's illustrate it with the following interval we wish to identify:

1. Assume for the moment that the bottom note of the interval is the first note of the major scale beginning on that note. In this example, the bottom note is G, so assume the G-major scale.

2. Identify the key signature for that scale. (If you don't know the key signature, look it up in parts 415-417.) The key signature for G-major is one sharp, F-sharp.

3. With the key signature we are ready to determine the quality of the third. IF THE TOP NOTE OF THE THIRD BELONGS TO THE MAJOR SCALE, IT IS A MAJOR THIRD. Or if you want to state it another way: IF THE TOP NOTE OF THE THIRD IS ONE-HALF STEP LOWER THAN CALLED FOR BY THE MAJOR SCALE, IT IS A MINOR THIRD. In our example, the interval is major, because the top note is naturally part of the G-major scale.

Please turn to part 228.

228

Two more examples of the process are given below:

What is the quality of this harmonic third—major or minor?

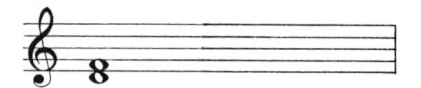

1. Assume the bottom note (D) begins the D-major scale.
2. Ascertain the key signature of D-major: two sharps, F♯ and C♯.
3. Is the top note of the interval (F) in the D-major scale?

    ANSWER: No; the D-major scale employs an F♯. The top note of the interval is an F-natural, which is one half step lower. The interval is, therefore, a MINOR third.

What is the quality of this melodic third—major or minor?

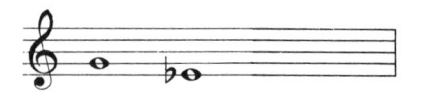

1. Assume the bottom note of this interval (E♭) begins the E♭-major scale.
2. What is the key signature of E♭-major? Three flats: B♭, E♭, A♭.
3. Is the top note of the interval (G) in the E♭-major scale?

    ANSWER: Yes, G falls naturally in the E♭-major scale, so the interval is a MAJOR third.

Now, try some exercises in major and minor thirds.

Use the Shield

Please identify this interval as major or minor.

The bottom note of the interval indicates we will employ which major scale?

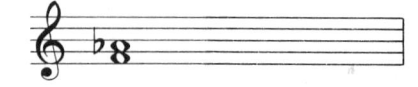

☙

F-major

Please turn to part 229.

Use the Shield

What is the key signature for F-major?

◈

One flat, B♭

Does the top note (A♭) of this third fall naturally in the F-major scale?

◈

No, in the F-major scale there is an A-natural. Our interval is one half step smaller, so the interval is a minor third.

Use the illustration to identify this third as major or minor.

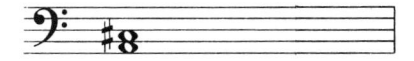

What scale will we employ in this bass clef example?

◈

A-major scale because the bottom note is A

What is the key signature for A-major?

◈

Three sharps, F♯, C♯, G♯

Is the C♯ (top note of the interval) in the A-major scale?

◈

Yes, one of the sharps in the key signature is C♯.

Is the interval major or minor in quality?

◈

It is a major third, because the top note of the interval is in the A-major scale.

Now return to part 226 and answer the Diagnostic Question.

230

You are right. A minor third is smaller than a major third by one half step.

The process of determining the quality of thirds is a bit complicated, but it has very wide applicability. Not only can you determine the quality of thirds, but the method works for all the following as well:

SECONDS of the major scale are major seconds.
FOURTHS of the major scale are perfect fourths.
FIFTHS of the major scale are perfect fifths.
SIXTHS of the major scale are major sixths.
SEVENTHS of the major scale are major sevenths.

You now have the capability of determining the quality of any interval in music through this one process. As you gain experience with the sounds of the intervals, their different sound qualities will be of further assistance. Turn to part 239.

231

Right: Now that you have identified the basic interval sizes, let's examine the different qualities of intervals. Turn to part 223.

232

A triad is composed of a third and a fifth (which you have already learned to identify), so learning the quality of triads will be easy.

C to E is a third. Remember that thirds are either major or minor. Because E is in the C-major scale, we know the third is major.

C to G is a fifth. Remember that fifths are either perfect, augmented, or diminished. Because G is in the C-major scale, we know the fifth is perfect.

If we combine the above intervals we have a triad with a major third and a perfect fifth. This is the makeup of a MAJOR TRIAD.

In this example, the smaller interval (E to G) is minor, and the larger interval (E to B) is a perfect fifth. This is the makeup of a MINOR TRIAD.

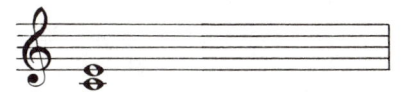

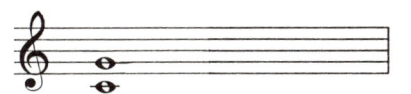

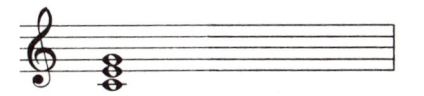

RULE: Triads contain a third and a fifth. The quality of the *third* determines the quality of the triad.

> perfect fifth } major triad
> major third
>
> perfect fifth } minor triad
> minor third

If you need to review the material on major and minor thirds, refer to part 227, but remember to return to this part before you continue the program.

Continue in part 240.

233

You chose the wrong alternative. You will find out why by reading the review in part 232.

234

It is easy to invert intervals. Simply put the bottom note of the interval on top as shown below.

In measure 1 you have the interval of a fifth, E to B. By moving the bottom E ABOVE the B to the closest line or space that is still E, you have inverted the interval. The interval in measure 2 is the inversion of the interval in 1.

Use the Shield

Write the inversion of this interval in the second measure.

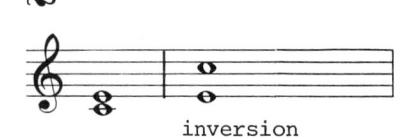

inversion

Write the inversion of this interval.

inversion

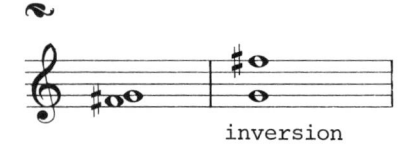

Please return to part 239 and answer the Diagnostic Question.

235

This Diagnostic Question tested your knowledge of chord inversions.

```
        1              2              3              4
      root position  first inversion  second inversion  root position
```

When a chord is built on three consecutive lines or spaces we call it a triad. We may also say it is in ROOT position (see measure 1 above). By moving the bottom note of the chord (in this case, D) to the top of the chord, the chord becomes a FIRST INVERSION, as illustrated in measure 2. If you invert it again by moving the new bottom note to the top, you create a SECOND INVERSION (measure 3). If you repeat the process still another time, you are back in root position again, but ONE OCTAVE HIGHER than the original position.

Use the Shield

This chord is an inversion. Write the chord in its root position in the second measure.

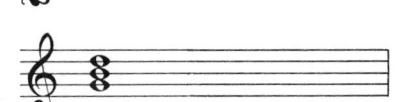

Here is a root position triad. Write its first inversion in the next measure.

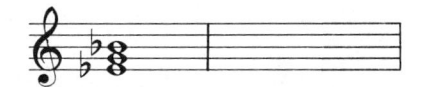

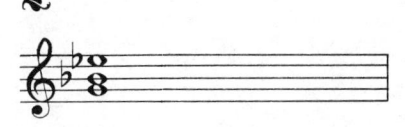

Now return to part 245 and answer the Diagnostic Question.

236

That alternative was incorrect. You can find out why in part 227.

237

Diagnostic Question Seven*

If three notes of a chord fall on consecutive lines or consecutive spaces, the chord formed is called a TRIAD.

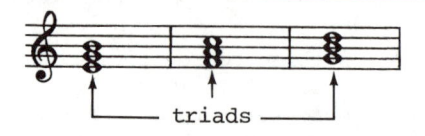

(musical staff showing triads)

By identifying the nature of the intervals of a triad, you can also determine whether the triad itself is major or minor.

Is the triad below a major or minor?

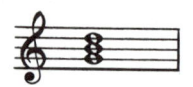

(musical staff showing a triad)

Alternatives

		part
a.	I'm not sure. I would like an explanation.	232
(b.)	major	242
c.	minor	233

238

You have made an error. An explanation of the concept can be found in part 232.

---

*If you have already answered this question, answer it correctly again and continue the program from the part indicated.

Diagnostic Question Six

The intervals on the left are INVERSIONS of which intervals on the right?

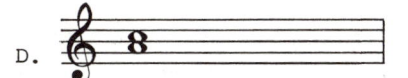

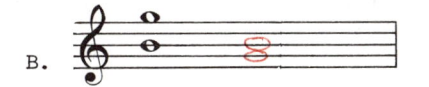

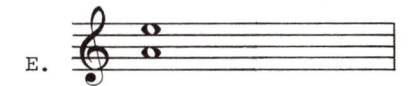

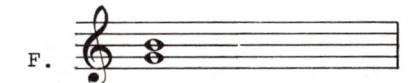

A.

B.

C.

D.

E.

F.

Alternatives

		part
1.	I am not familiar with the musical meaning of inversion.	234
2.	A is the inversion of E B is the inversion of F C is the inversion of D	246
3.	A is the inversion of F B is the inversion of D C is the inversion of E	241
4.	A is the inversion of E B is the inversion of D C is the inversion of F	224

240

Use the Shield

In this example, the bottom third is major, the fifth is perfect. Is the triad major or minor?

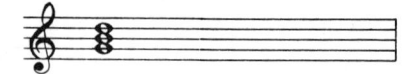

∾

major

Is this triad major or minor?

∾

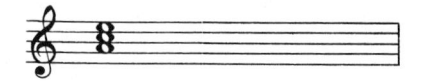

minor (The bottom third is minor.)

What two intervals make up a minor triad?

∾

A minor third in the bottom interval, and a perfect fifth in the largest interval.

Is this triad major or minor?

∾

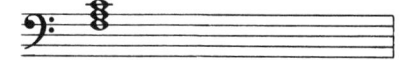

major (The bottom interval is major.)

Now return to the Diagnostic Question in part 237.

241

No, you must have slipped up. For an explanation go to part 234.

242

Yes, the chord is a major triad. If the notes of a chord fall on three consecutive lines or spaces, it is a triad. A triad is made up of a bottom interval (a third) and a larger interval (always a perfect fifth). If the bottom third is major, the triad is major. If the bottom third is minor, the triad is minor.

perfect fifth   major third   perfect fifth   minor third

Now try the Diagnostic Question in part 243.

243

Diagnostic Question Eight

Which of the following triads are CORRECTLY marked?

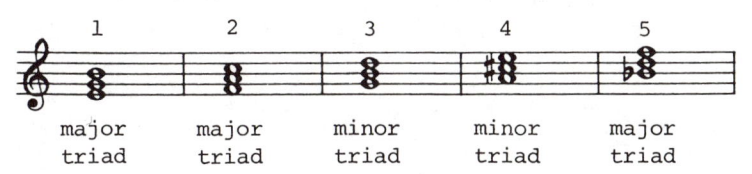

1	2	3	4	5
major triad	major triad	minor triad	minor triad	major triad

Alternatives

		part
a.	May I review this concept?	232
b.	1 and 4 are correct.	238
c.	3 and 5 are correct.	247
d.	2 and 5 are correct.	245

244

Were you misled by the fact that those three chords all had the same notes, except for the sharp and flat? Please read the explanation in part 235.

245

Exactly. You have learned to identify some major and minor triads. Although many other chords exist in music, our discussion is limited to these important basic ones.

Diagnostic Question Nine

Of the chords shown below, three comprise a root chord and its first two inversions. Which are they?

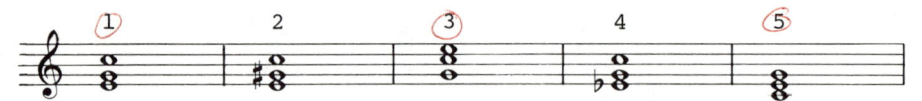

Alternatives

	part
1. I'm not sure of the meaning of inversion as applied to this example. Please explain.	235
2. Chords 1, 2, and 4.	244
3. Chords 1, 3, and 5.	248

246

Yes, you have selected the right inversion for each interval. Several things about inversions are consistent, and make them easier to work with. The graph and the two points below are most important.

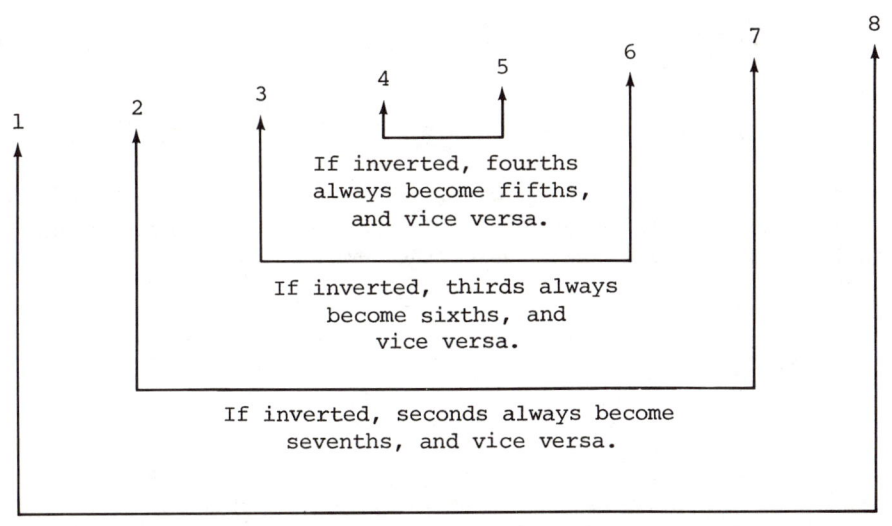

```
  1     2     3     4     5     6     7     8
  ↑     ↑     ↑     ↑     ↑     ↑     ↑     ↑
              |     |     |     |
              |     └─────┘     |
              |  If inverted,   |
              |  fourths always |
              |  become fifths, |
              |  and vice versa.|
              |                 |
              └─────────────────┘
              If inverted, thirds always
                become sixths, and
                    vice versa.
        
        If inverted, seconds always become
            sevenths, and vice versa.

        If inverted, octaves always remain octaves.
```

If you invert any major interval, the new interval always becomes minor, and vice versa (e.g., a major third becomes a minor sixth).

If you invert any perfect interval, the new interval remains perfect (e.g., a perfect fourth becomes a perfect fifth).

The next step of the program is to form chords of three notes.

Go to part 237.

247

You seem to be confused about something. A review begins in 232.

248

Correct. The chords you chose were inversions of one another. Triads exist in ROOT POSITION, FIRST INVERSION, and SECOND INVERSION as shown below.

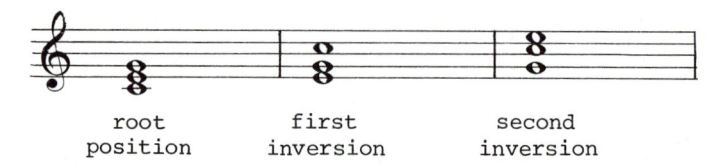

root position   first inversion   second inversion

Triads can be built on every note of the scale. The example below includes triads built on notes of the C-major scale.

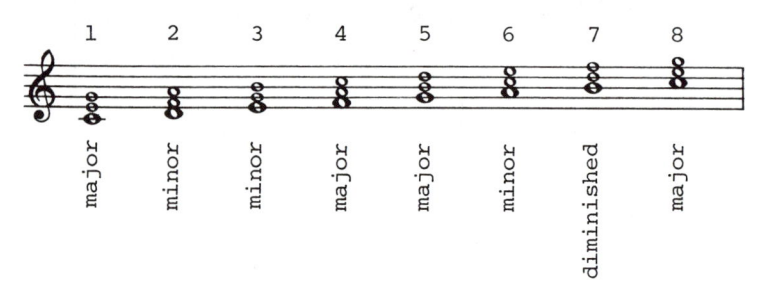

1 — major
2 — minor
3 — minor
4 — major
5 — major
6 — minor
7 — diminished
8 — major

Use the Shield

Examine the chords above. Which of these chords are major?

𝄋

Only chords 1, 4, 5, and 8 are major.

Put the Shield Aside

Did you notice that chord 8 is the same as chord 1? It is merely one octave higher. The chords 1, 4, and 5 are the *primary* chords in any major key. They are designated by the upper-case roman numerals I, IV, and V to indicate that they are major chords. The chords of secondary importance are 2, 3, and 6. These chords are designated with lower-case roman numerals to indicate their minor nature as follows: ii, iii, vi. (The vii chord has special characteristics that will not be discussed here.)

Please turn to part 249.

Use the Shield

If you form a major scale on any note, will the triads on notes 1, 4, and 5 of the scale always be major?

☙

Certainly. The I, IV, and V chords of all major keys are major.

On the staff directly below, which chords are major?

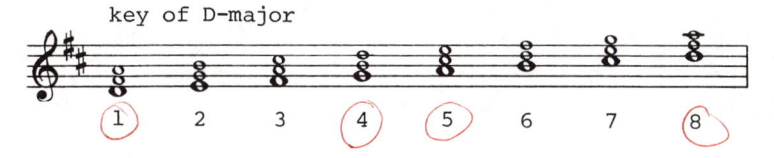

key of D-major

☙

Chords 1, 4, and 5, i.e., the chords on notes D, G, and A are major in the D-major scale. (Don't forget the sharps.)

Which chords are major in this scale?

key of F-major

☙

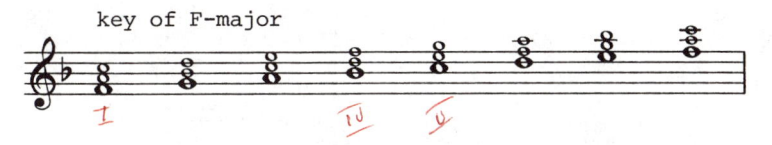

The chords on notes F, B♭, and C are major. They are found on notes 1, 4, and 5 of the F-major scale. (Remember, the B on note 4 is B♭, as indicated by the flat in the key signature.)

Which chords are major in this scale?

key of E-major

☙

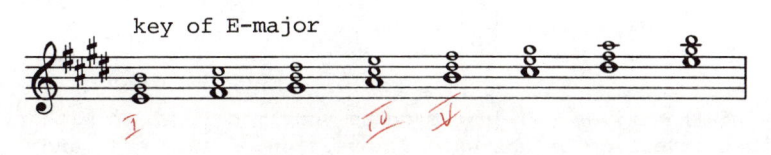

The chords on notes E, A, and B.

Congratulations! You have now completed chapter 4. You will find several helpful Proficiency Developers in the next part. Be sure to do them. They will help refine the knowledge you have just acquired.

Please turn to part 250.

250

Proficiency Developers

1. Five intervals are shown below. Draw the inversion of each in the empty measures provided.

   A.

   B.

   C.

   D.

   E.

2. Shown below are several intervals of a third. Determine the quality (major or minor) of each interval. You may review the process in part 227 if needed. All key signatures are found in parts 415-417.

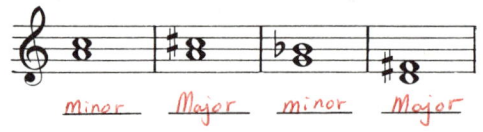

   minor   Major   minor   Major

3. In the measures shown below, construct a major triad on each of the notes given.

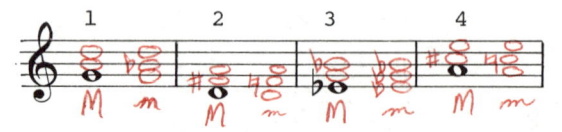

   M m   M m   M m   M m

4. Using the triads you just made as your model, write either the first inversion or the second inversion of each one, and label it correctly.

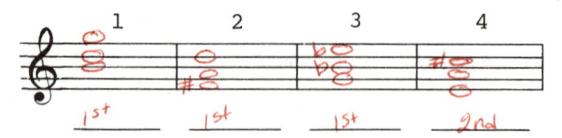

   1st   1st   1st   2nd

5. Return to the triads in number 3 and change them to minor triads by reducing the size of the bottom third one half step.

Turn to part 251.

251

AMERICA THE BEAUTIFUL

Samuel A. Ward

1. O beau-ti-ful for spa-cious skies, For am-ber waves of grain, For pur-ple moun-tain maj-es-ties A-bove the fruit-ed plain. A-mer-i-ca! A-mer-i-ca! God shed His grace on thee, And
2. O beau-ti-ful for pil-grim feet Whose stern im-pas-sion'd stress A thor-ough-fare for free-dom beat A-cross the wil-der-ness. A-mer-i-ca! A-mer-i-ca! God mend thine ev'-ry flaw, Con
3. O beau-ti-ful for he-roes prov'd In lib-er-at-ing strife, Who more than self their coun-try loved, And mer-cy more than life. A-mer-i-ca! A-mer-i-ca! May God thy gold re-fine Till
4. O beau-ti-ful for pa-triot dream That sees be-yond the years Thine al-a-bas-ter cit-ies gleam Un-dimmed by hu-man tears. A-mer-i-ca! A-mer-i-ca! God shed His grace on thee, And

Go to part 252.

252

AMERICA THE BEAUTIFUL

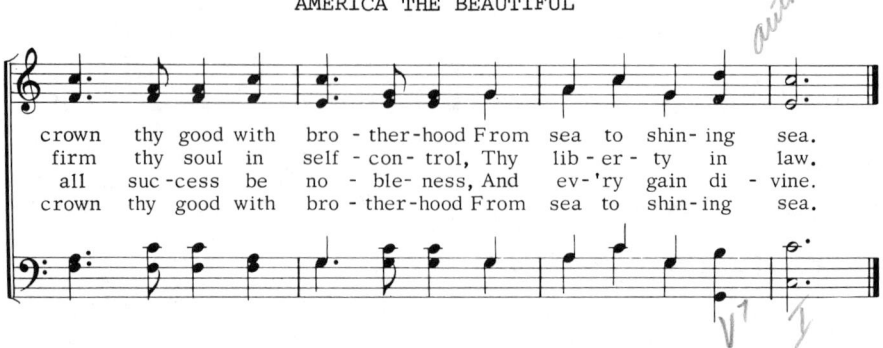

crown thy good with bro-ther-hood From sea to shin-ing sea.
firm thy soul in self-con-trol, Thy lib-er-ty in law.
all suc-cess be no-ble-ness, And ev-'ry gain di-vine.
crown thy good with bro-ther-hood From sea to shin-ing sea.

6. Practice singing the melody of "America the Beautiful" by yourself. If possible, play the first note on an instrument so you can sing it at the pitch in which it is written.

7. Practice harmony by singing the alto, tenor, or bass part of "America the Beautiful" several times. You may need to play the part slowly on an instrument to help you learn it.

8. Point at different intervals in the song at random and identify their sizes. If the interval is a third, identify its quality.

   Here are two supportive skills that may be helpful to you.

   1. If you have real difficulty figuring out the quality of a third, try counting the number of whole steps in the interval. Major thirds always contain TWO WHOLE STEPS, and minor thirds contain one whole step and one half step.

   2. There is a quick way to identify thirds of triads. We have learned to identify the bottom third and the fifth in a triad, but another third is present (see the example below).

IN A MAJOR THIRD, THE TOP THIRD IS ALWAYS MINOR. IN A MINOR TRIAD, THE TOP THIRD IS ALWAYS MAJOR.

In other words, <u>the quality of the top third in a triad is the opposite quality from the triad itself.</u>

Go to part 253.

253

9. Look at the song, "The Magic of Christmas." Can you find any melodic thirds or fourths in the melody? Circle them. What harmonic intervals are most common in the accompaniment? Try singing or playing the melody. Then sing it as a round.

THE MAGIC OF CHRISTMAS*

Spirited   (In two)   Laurence & Donna Lyon

See the mag-ic of Christ-mas glist-'ning in the snow.

2.
Feel the mag-ic of Christ-mas in the fi-re's glow.

3.
Chil-dren whis-per of San-ta, Stock-ings hung in a row.

Continued on the following page.

*Used with permission, A. Laurence Lyon, Oregon College of Education, Monmouth, Oregon.

4.

Hear the bells ring; Car-ol-ers sing of long a - go.

Now, turn to the Self-Test in part 254.

Self-Test

You are now ready to evaluate your understanding of the material in chapter 4, so you can determine the concepts to review. When considering intervals, you may use the keyboard on the shield if you so desire.

Match the three terms with the proper definition on the right.

1. chord *B*
2. interval *C*
3. triad *A*

A. a chord with the notes placed on three consecutive lines or spaces

B. a combination of notes that are sounded together

C. the difference in pitch between two notes played simultaneously or consecutively

Identify each interval on the staff below by writing its size (i.e., second, third, fourth, etc.) underneath.

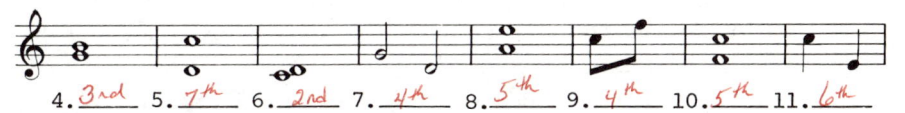

4. *3rd* 5. *7th* 6. *2nd* 7. *4th* 8. *5th* 9. *4th* 10. *5th* 11. *6th*

Which of the following intervals are either perfect, augmented, or diminished?

12. *B*

A. second and thirds
B. fourths and fifths
C. sixths and sevenths

Identify the intervals on the staff below as major or minor thirds and write your answers underneath.

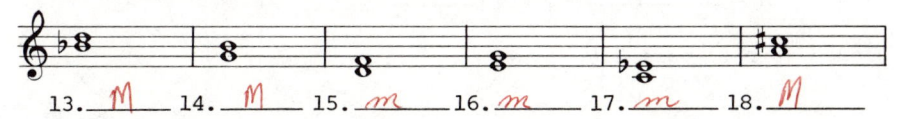

13. *M* 14. *M* 15. *m* 16. *m* 17. *m* 18. *M*

19. These two intervals are the same in all ways but one. How are they different?

harmonic   *melodic*

Turn to part 255.

20. What two intervals are necessary to create a major triad? _major third_ and _perfect fifth_
21. What two intervals are necessary to create a minor triad? _minor third_ and _perfect fifth_

Identify each of the following triads as major or minor.

22. _M_   23. _m_   24. _M_   25. _M_

26. Construct a triad on each note in the staff. Then, write its first inversion in the next measure.

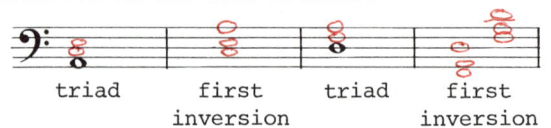

    triad   first   triad   first
              inversion   inversion

27. Which chords in a major key are called the primary chords? _I IV V_

28. What is the quality of each of the primary chords in major keys? _Major_

29. Write in the notes needed to complete the primary chords in the two following scales.

    key of B♭-major   key of E-major

30. In "America the Beautiful" (part 251), how many harmonic intervals of a third are there in the treble clef? How many in the bass clef?
    treble: _25_ bass: _5_

Please turn to part 256.

Now check your answers with those in the key that follows. Be sure to review all questions immediately by referring to the part indicated in the Review Index. If you missed a substantial number of questions you probably need to review the chapter. Go through it again, carefully choosing your answers to the Diagnostic Questions. Then go on to chapter 5, part 257.

Answers & Review Index

1. B (chord defined 208)
2. C (interval defined 213)
3. A (triad defined 237)
4. 3rd (interval size 219)
5. 7th (interval size 219)
6. 2nd (interval size 219)
7. 4th (interval size 219)
8. 5th (interval size 219)
9. 4th (interval size 219)
10. 5th (interval size 219)
11. 6th (interval size 219)
12. B (perfect fourths and fifths 225)
13. major third (quality of thirds 227 ff)
14. major third (quality of thirds 227 ff)
15. minor third (quality of thirds 227 ff)
16. minor third (quality of thirds 227 ff)
17. minor third (quality of thirds 227 ff)
18. major third (quality of thirds 227 ff)
19. The first measure is a *harmonic* interval, the second is a *melodic* interval (harmonic and melodic intervals 213)
20. A major third on the bottom, and a perfect fifth. Or if you are following the rule mentioned in the Proficiency Developers, a major third for the bottom interval and a minor third for the top interval. (quality of triads 232, 252)
21. A minor third on the bottom, and a perfect fifth. (quality of triads 232, 252)
22. major (quality of triads 232)
23. minor (quality of triads 232)
24. major (quality of triads 232)

25. major (quality of triads 232 ff)

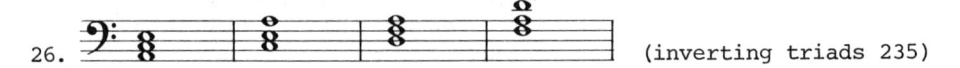

26. [bass clef staff with triads] (inverting triads 235)

27. The I, IV, and V chords (primary chords in any key 247 ff)
28. They are all major triads (quality of primary chords 247 ff)
29.

[treble clef staff with I IV V chords in two keys]

(primary chords 248 ff)

30. Treble clef: 25 thirds; bass clef: 5 thirds (interval size 219)

5
Major Scales, Chords, and Keys

257

For many years, traditional Western music has been dominated by a system of harmony known as TERTIAN, i.e., based on the interval of a third. Understanding of tertian harmony requires knowledge of scales, chords, keys, and key tones—the subjects of this chapter.

Objectives

1. Recognize definitions of key, key tone, scale, tonality, and cadence.
2. Recall at what places in major scales the half steps are located.
3. Recall some characteristic relationships of the notes of the major scale, particularly notes 1, 2, 5, and 7.
4. Recall the syllabic names of the notes in the TONIC SOL-FA system.
5. Determine key signatures by using a "circle of fifths" diagram.
6. Demonstrate knowledge of the keys of C, D, B-flat, and A-major as follows:

   Concerning the scale of each key:
   a. Illustrate where the half steps fall in each scale.
   b. Recognize the key signature for each key.
   c. Identify the most important notes in each scale by name.

   Concerning chords in each key:
   a. Recognize the names of the chords.
   b. Identify some major characteristics of the I, IV, and V chords.
   c. Recall possible substitutes for the I, IV, and V chords.

7. Determine the seventh note that makes a V chord a V_7 chord.

Go to part 258.

8. Recall three common cadential patterns (chord patterns that form cadences).

To discuss harmony intelligently, you must understand these musical terms:

1. KEY: a system of tones that are drawn to a central tone, and bear the name of the central tone (e.g., key of F).
2. KEY TONE: the central tone to which other tones are drawn; where complete resolution is found.
3. SCALE: a series of tones in ascending or descending order, beginning with the key tone, and maintaining fixed distances between all tones.
4. TONALITY: the organization of tones around a key tone.
5. CADENCE: a series of chords that conveys the impression of conclusion.

Before proceeding with this chapter, be sure you understand these definitions. They will be required of you later in the program. There are five Diagnostic Questions in this chapter.

Use the Shield

In the discussion of scales in chapter 3, you learned that whole steps exist between most of the notes of the major scale, but that half steps exist between tones _____ to _____, and _____ to _____ .

❧

As shown on the keyboard below, half steps exist between tones 3 to 4, and 7 to 8 of the major scale. All other steps are whole steps. This is true of all major keys.

C-major scale

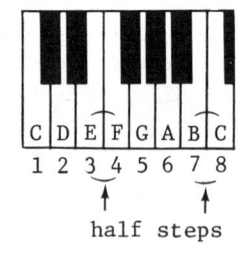

```
C D E F G A B C
1 2 3 4 5 6 7 8
    ↑       ↑
   half steps
```

Turn to part 259.

259

Diagnostic Question One

In the key of C, the key tone is C; in the key of D, it is D, and so on. The key tone is always the first (1) and last (8) tone of any scale. Beginning with the key tone, the notes of the scale are numbered 1 through 8 in ascending order.

From the alternatives below, choose the one that correctly matches the tone with its number IN THE KEY OF G-MAJOR. (You may use the keyboard facsimile on the back of the shield if you wish.)

Alternatives

		part
a.	Could I see the review before selecting an answer?	261
b.	D = 5, C = 4, G = 1, E = 6	282
c.	D = 2, C = 1, G = 5, E = 3	264
d.	D = 4, C = 3, G = 1, E = 6	279

260

That's right. When you are unsure about a key signature, it is not always possible (or desirable) to look it up in the circle of fifths, so the most frequently used key signatures should be committed to memory as soon as possible. The key signature is used to place the half steps at the proper places in the scale. All key signatures and scales are shown in the Appendix at the end of the book.

Go to part 273.

261

Here is the review. When numbering the tones in any scale, give the key tone the first number. For the key of G, the key tone is G. For the key of F, it is F. Using the key of F as an example, the notes of the F-major scale are numbered as follows:

```
F G A B♭ C D E F
1 2 3 4  5 6 7 8
```

If you examine the intervals between steps 3 to 4 and 7 to 8, you will see that a flat must be added to the B to make a major scale. However, that addition does not affect the position (or numbers) of the notes within the scale.

Use the Shield

In the key of A-major, what are the numbers of D, F♯, and G♯?

🙰

4, 6, 7: A B C♯ D E F♯ G♯ A
         1 2 3 4 5 6 7 8

In the key of F-major, what are the numbers of notes G, A, and E?

🙰

2, 3, 7

In the key of D-major, what numbers are notes E, G, and A?

🙰

2, 4, 5

Return to the question in part 259.

262

That was not the correct alternative. Please go on to part 278.

263

Certainly. The chords match as follows:

<u>Tonic, the I chord</u>. This chord includes the key tone and is the fundamental chord of any key.

<u>Dominant, the V chord</u>. This chord is the one most used for departure from the tonic chord. It is second to the tonic chord in importance.

<u>Subdominant, the IV chord</u>. This is one of the three major chords in any major key. Although widely used, it is not as important to the key as the dominant chord.

Thus far, we have not discussed the chords on the other tones of the major scale except to say that three are minor and are, therefore, designated with lower-case numerals.

Although the following generalization is deceptive because it is not always true, it is worth mentioning. Each of the three major chords (I, IV, and V) has a minor substitute as follows:

```
       chord:  I   IV   V
  substitute:  vi  ii   iii
```

The above substitutions should not generally be made in a cadence, particularly the iii for V. Otherwise, the minor chords may occasionally be substituted for, used in front of, or following the related major chords with pleasant results. Notice that the root tone of each substitute chord is located a minor third below the root tone of the respective major chord. The substitutes are, therefore, termed the relative MINOR CHORDS of their respective major chords. Minor scales built on their root tones are RELATIVE MINOR SCALES, which will be discussed in chapter 6.

Now go to part 287.

264

No, let's look at the problem again. Turn to part 261.

265

Use the Shield

In the D-major scale (shown below), the note E will tend to resolve to note ___D (1)___ , and C-sharp will tend to resolve to ___D (8)___ .

$$D \quad E \quad F\sharp \quad G \quad A \quad B \quad C\sharp \quad D$$

❧

D (1) and D (8)

In the D-major scale, what is the name of the fifth tone that can jump down to 1 or up to 8 equally well? ___A___

❧

A

In any major scale, the second tone tends to resolve (*up/down*) ~~down~~ and the seventh tone tends to resolve ___up___ .

❧

down, up

The fifth tone is the second most important note of the scale; only the first tone is more important. The fifth tone is the main point of departure in the scale and resolves (*up to 8/down to 1*). ___Both___

❧

Both! The fifth tone may resolve either direction.

Go to part 267.

266

That wasn't quite right. Go on to part 272.

Many musicians prefer to give the tones of the scale syllabic names rather than numbers because syllables are much easier to sing. This system of syllables, known as the TONIC SOL-FA, or MOVABLE DO system, has been widely used for many years. Most children become acquainted with the symbols in grade school. The names of the notes are identified below. (The scale is usually read from the bottom up, and may seem most familiar to you that way.)

```
        Scale Number          Syllable

              8 . . . . . . . Do
              7 . . . . . . . Ti
              6 . . . . . . . La
              5 . . . . . . . Sol
              4 . . . . . . . Fa
              3 . . . . . . . Mi
              2 . . . . . . . Re
              1 . . . . . . . Do
```

Use the Shield

The first and eighth tones of the scale are both called __Do__ in this system.

☙

do

The fifth tone of the scale is __Sol__ and resolves either direction to *do* (both 1 and 8 are *do*).

☙

sol

In the C-major scale, the note E has the syllabic name __Mi__ .

☙

mi

In the G-major scale, the note E has the syllabic name __la__ .

☙

la

Turn to part 268.

By now it must be apparent that there are many major keys and scales. The diagram below depicts all major scales and the number of sharps or flats in each of their key signatures. If you begin at the top and follow around the right side of the circle, you will see that each new key is the interval of a fifth above the previous key, and adds one sharp to the previous key signature. Going the opposite direction, each new key adds one flat. At the bottom, ==G♭-major and F♯-major== are labeled **ENHARMONIC KEYS**, because they consist of exactly the same notes, but the notes are identified by different names.

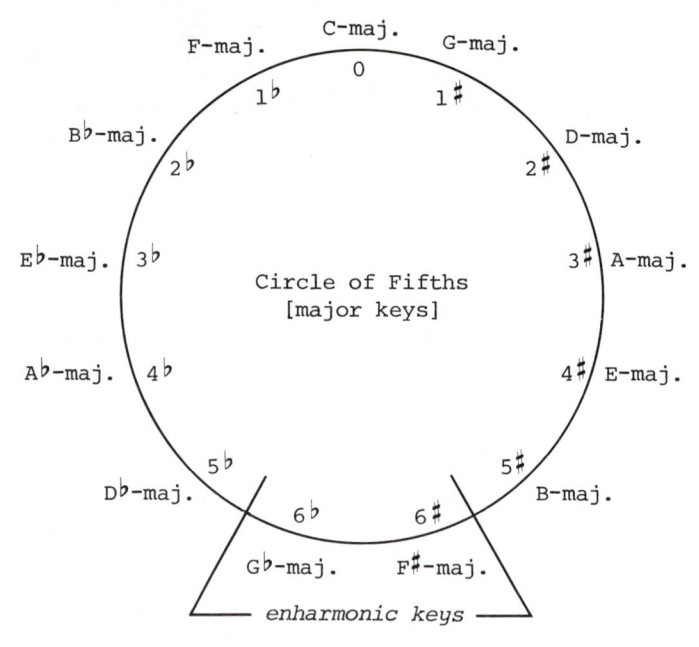

```
                    C-maj.
         F-maj.       0      G-maj.
                 1♭       1♯
    B♭-maj.                       D-maj.
             2♭              2♯

 E♭-maj.   3♭                  3♯   A-maj.
                Circle of Fifths
                  [major keys]
 A♭-maj.   4♭                  4♯   E-maj.

             5♭              5♯
    D♭-maj.                       B-maj.
                 6♭       6♯
                G♭-maj.  F♯-maj.
                 enharmonic keys
```

In any key signature involving sharps, the sharps always appear in the following order: F♯, C♯, G♯, D♯, A♯, and E♯. For example:
—If the key signature is 1♯, it will always be F♯.
—If the key signature is 2♯, they will always be F♯ and C♯.
—If the key signature is 3♯, they will always be F♯, C♯, and G♯. And so on, through all six sharps.

Likewise, in key signatures involving flats, the flats always appear in the following order: B♭, E♭, A♭, D♭, G♭, C♭.

Many people feel it is important to memorize the order of sharps and flats because it helps them determine key signatures.

Please turn to part 269.

269

You may also determine key signatures as follows:

FLATS: Reading from left to right, the *next to last* flat in the key signature bears the name of the key.

(In this example it is E♭.)

SHARPS: Reading from left to right, the key note is one half step above the last sharp in the signature. (In this example the last sharp is D♯, so the key is E.)

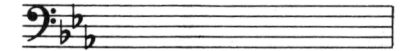

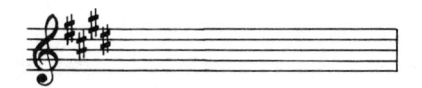

Here are two more examples:

In example 1, the next to last flat is A-flat; the key is A-flat major. In example 2, the last sharp is A-sharp; the note directly above A-sharp is B, so the key is B-major.

Please continue to part 270.

270

Diagnostic Question Two

Pictured below are three key signatures. Identify each and choose the correct alternative.

Alternatives

		part
a.	I am unsure of this concept. Please explain.	272
b.	1 = B♭-major 2 = D-major 3 = A-major	260
c.	1 = A-major 2 = B♭-major 3 = D-major	266
d.	1 = D-major 2 = A-major 3 = B♭-major	276

271

No, you have matched the wrong items. For an explanation, turn to part 285.

It is not necessary to recognize all key signatures and remember their names, although this ability is beneficial. It is important, however, to be able to determine key signatures by applying the procedures discussed in part 269, or by looking them up in the circle of fifths (part 268). Using one of those methods, answer the following questions.

Use the Shield

What key signature has four sharps?

☙

E-major

What key signature has five flats?

☙

D♭-major

What key signature has two sharps?

☙

D-major

What key does this signature indicate?

☙

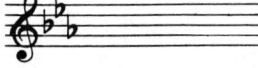

E♭-major

What key does this signature indicate?

☙

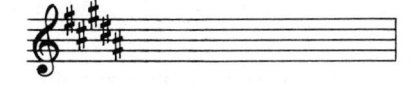

B-major

Now return to the question in part 270.

Use the Shield

The B-flat major key signature consists of how many flats? 2 B♭E♭

❧

two (B-flat and E-flat)

The A-major key signature consists of how many sharps or flats? F C G

❧

three sharps (F-sharp, C-sharp, and G-sharp)

The key signature for D-major consists of how many sharps or flats? F C

❧

two sharps (F-sharp and C-sharp)

A-major has three sharps. They are __F__ , __C__ , and __G__ .

❧

F-sharp, C-sharp, and G-sharp

D-major has two sharps. They are __F__ and __C__ .

❧

F-sharp and C-sharp

A-major has the same sharps as D-major plus one more, namely, __G__ .

❧

G-sharp

In B-flat major, the two flats are __B♭__ , and __E♭__ .

❧

B-flat, E-flat

Turn to part 274.

274

It may be necessary to use a piano keyboard to determine the following answers. It will certainly be necessary to remember which sharps or flats are included in the keys under consideration.

Use the Shield

In the key of A-major, note names 1, 4, and 5 are __A__, __D__, and __E__.

☙

A, D, E

In B-flat major, notes 1, 4, and 5 are __B♭__, __E♭__, and __F__.

☙

B-flat, E-flat, F

In D-major, notes 2, 3, and 7 are __E__, __F#__, and __C#__.

☙

E, F-sharp, C-sharp

In B-flat major, notes 2, 3, and 7 are __C__, __D__, and __A__.

☙

C, D, A

In A-major, notes 2, 5, and 7 are __B__, __E__, and __G#__.

☙

B, E, G-sharp

In any scale the most important tone is number __1__, and the second most important tone is __5__.

☙

Tone 1 is most important, and 5 is next in importance.

Go to part 275.

275

So far we have identified the notes of the scale with numbers (1-8) and syllables (sol-fa). Each note of the scale also has a name that is frequently used to identify the chord or triad built on that tone. These note or chord names are identified below on the C-major scale.

The names, particularly those of the I, IV, and V chords, are important to you, and should be learned. They will be required later in the program.

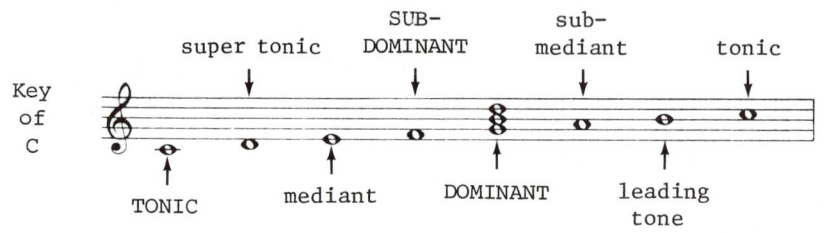

Key of C:
- TONIC
- super tonic
- mediant
- SUB-DOMINANT
- DOMINANT
- sub-mediant
- leading tone
- tonic

Any triad built on one of the above notes will carry the same name as that note. A chord has been constructed on G, the DOMINANT TONE of the scale. In C-major, the chord is, therefore, known as the dominant chord or triad. A chord built on any other note of that scale will also carry that respective name. It is imperative to remember that the chord names for particular notes change when keys change. For instance, the chord built on G in the example above is the DOMINANT CHORD in the key of C. In the key of G (see the example below), G is the key tone or the TONIC NOTE and the chord is the TONIC CHORD. Although the tonic chord in the key of G possesses exactly the same notes as the dominant chord in the key of C, it serves a different function in the new key.

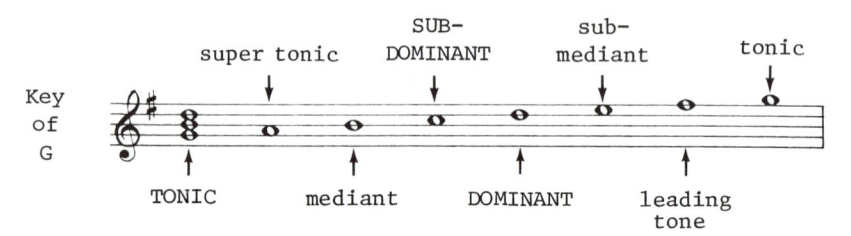

Key of G:
- TONIC
- super tonic
- mediant
- SUB-DOMINANT
- DOMINANT
- sub-mediant
- leading tone
- tonic

Go to part 277.

276

That wasn't quite right. Please continue in part 272.

Just as the first and fifth tones are the most important tones of the scale, the chords built on these tones are the most important chords. They are the I or TONIC chord, and the V or DOMINANT chord. The tonic chord is the fundamental chord of the key—the "home" chord where resolution is achieved in most music. Notice that the dominant chord possesses not only the fifth tone of the scale (which may move either up or down to the tonic), but tones 2 and 7 as well. Remember, tone 2 leads down to 1, and 7 leads up to 8. The chord is, therefore, quite dominant in its effort to resolve to the tonic. It is also the most commonly used chord for departure from the tonic chord.

In chapter 4, you learned that the I, IV, and V chords (tonic, subdominant, and dominant chords) are the only three major chords in any major key. The subdominant chord is not as important as the dominant and tonic chords, but because of its major quality and its use in traditional Western music it can be considered the third most important chord in any given key. The importance of knowing these three chords in several keys cannot be over-emphasized. They are the basis of many songs, and may be used to accompany them.

Diagnostic Question Three

From the alternatives below, choose the one that correctly identifies the I, IV, and V chords in the key of A-major.

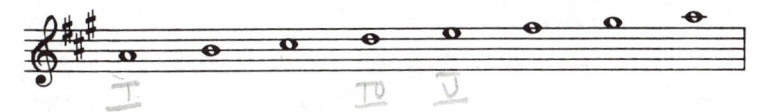

Alternatives

		part
a.	I would like to see the review first.	278
b.	I chord = A, C, E IV chord = D, F, A V chord = E, G, B	283
c.	I chord = A, C♯, E IV chord = D, F♯, A V chord = E, G♯, B	280
d.	I chord = A, C♯, E IV chord = D♯, F, A V chord = E, G, B♯	262

Here is a review of how to identify the notes in the I, IV, and V chords of any given key.

Let's take the key of E-flat major as an example. It has three flats: B-flat, E-flat, and A-flat. The key tone is, of course, E-flat. By writing the notes of that scale on the staff below, we can begin our analysis.

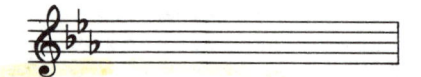

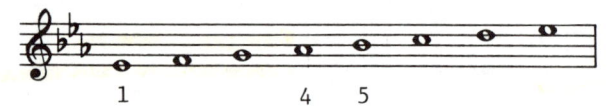

The next step is to mark notes 1, 4, and 5, thereby identifying the notes on which the tonic, subdominant, and dominant chords will be built.

The notes in any triad fall on consecutive lines or spaces, whichever the case may be. As seen above, the I chord begins on the bottom line (E-flat). It will, therefore, include the next two lines (G and B-flat). The IV chord begins on the second space up (A-flat), and includes the next two spaces (C and E-flat). The V chord begins on the third line from the bottom (B-flat) and includes the next two lines (D and F).

Briefly, here are the steps just used:

1. Identify the key signature and put it on the staff.

2. Write in the notes of the scale and identify notes 1, 4, and 5.

3. Determine the notes of each triad by identifying the two consecutive lines or spaces above the first, fourth, and fifth notes.

Use the Shield

What are the notes of the I chord and V chord in B-flat major?

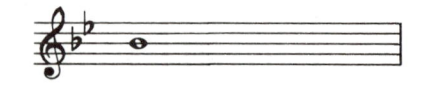

I = B♭, D, F; V = F, A, C. The I chord starts on the key tone (B-flat), as shown on the right. The V chord starts five notes higher, on F.

Go back to part 277 and answer the Diagnostic Question.

279

Oops, let's look again. Go to part 261.

280

Naturally. By being careful, it is easy to determine the I, IV, and V chords. Here are a few more examples for practice, but remember:

 I = tonic
 IV = subdominant
 V = dominant

Use the Shield

In A-major, the tonic chord consists of which notes?

༄

A, C-sharp, E (Watch the sharps!)

In B-flat major, the notes of the dominant chord are _____ , _____ , _____ .

༄

F, A, C (Count up five notes from B-flat, then add the next two spaces. B♭ counts as note 1.)

In D-major, the subdominant chord is made up of _____ , _____ , _____ .

༄

G, B, D (Count up four notes from D, then add the next two lines.)

In C-major, the dominant chord has _____ , _____ , and _____ .

༄

G, B, D (Count up five notes from C, then add the next two lines.)

Please turn to part 281.

Diagnostic Question Four

In the three columns below, the name, number, and characteristics of three chords are given. Match the items in the three columns, and choose the correct alternative from those at the bottom of the page. (Your answer will be something like A-2-X.)

A. dominant   1. IV chord   X. This chord is based on the key tone. It is the fundamental chord of any key.

B. tonic   2. V chord   Y. This chord is the most used chord for departure from the home chord. It is second to the home chord in importance.

C. subdominant   3. I chord   Z. This is one of the three major chords in a major key. Although widely used, it is not as important to the key as the chord described in Y above.

Alternatives

		part
a.	Please provide an explanation.	285
b.	A-2-X B-3-Z C-1-Y	271
c.	A-2-Y B-3-Z C-1-X	286
d.	A-2-Y B-3-X C-1-Z	263

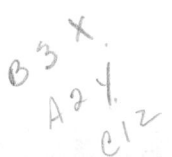

282

Precisely. In the G-major scale (or any other scale), tone 1 falls on the key tone and the other tones follow in order.

```
G A B C D E F# G
1 2 3 4 5 6 7  8
```

The definition of a key tone stated that other tones in the key are drawn toward that tone. This is true with different degrees of intensity for different tones. The key tone is tone 1, or 8, and is the "home" tone where the aural sense of conclusion or "arrival" is achieved. Tone 7 is strongly drawn up to tone 8, and tone 2 is drawn down to tone 1, as shown below.

```
1 2 3 4 5 6 7 8
```

Tone 7 is drawn to 8 with greater intensity than any other tone. One reason for this effect is that it is just one half step from the key tone and very much under its influence.

Because of western musical tradition (and acoustical reasons that will not be discussed here), the fifth tone of the scale is used as the main point of departure from the key tone. Tone 5 may resolve with equal ease either up to tone 8 or down to tone 1 (as shown below), falling a fifth to 1, or jumping a fourth to 8.

```
1 2 3 4 5 6 7 8
```

Other tones in the scale (tones 3, 4, and 6) also tend to follow certain patterns of progression, but the tones of main importance are those mentioned and illustrated in the preceding diagram.

Go to part 265.

283

That was not correct. Please read the explanation in part 278.

284

That was not the correct alternative. Please read the brief explanation in part 291.

285

Here is the explanation.

The tonic chord (I) is the fundamental chord of the key and is built on the first note of the scale. Toward this chord, most music "strives"; when it is reached, a feeling of conclusion or finality is achieved. The tonic chord, therefore, has been identified as the HOME chord.

The dominant chord (V) is the second strongest chord in any key. When composers want to progress from the tonic chord to another chord, they usually progress through the dominant chord, even if they go through several other chords on the way. It is the most common chord of departure from the tonic.

The subdominant chord (IV) is the third of the three major chords in any major key. Its quality ranks it among the three strongest chords, but it holds a less important position than the I and V chords.

To summarize:

I is the tonic, the strongest chord in the key; built on the key tone; a chord of conclusion.

IV is the subdominant, the third strongest chord in the key; built on the fourth tone of the scale; a secondary chord of departure from I.

V is the dominant, the second strongest chord in the key; built on the fifth tone of the scale; primary chord of departure from I.

Return to the Diagnostic Question in part 281 and see if you can now answer it correctly.

286

No, you have matched the wrong items. For pertinent information, go to part 285.

Use the Shield

A substitute for the I chord could be the __vi__ chord.

vi   (down 2 steps from 1 or 8)

A substitute for the IV chord could be the __ii__ chord.

ii   (down 2 steps from 4)

A substitute for the V chord could be the __iii__ chord.

iii

The relative minor of the I chord is the __vi__ chord.

vi

The relative minor of the V chord is the __iii__ chord.

iii

The relative minor of the IV chord is the __ii__ chord.

ii

Turn to part 288.

288

The V chord has one other characteristic that deserves attention. It is frequently referred to as the V_7 (five-seven) chord when the TONE ON THE SEVENTH STEP of that chord is added. See the following example in the key of C-major.

From the root tone of this chord (G), the new tone is seven steps away. When the new tone is added, the chord is known as a V_7 or DOMINANT-SEVENTH chord. The new tone is always added on the next consecutive line or space. Its addition increases the chord's "feeling of restlessness" and its demand for resolution to the tonic chord.

seventh step above the root tone
← first tone
key of C-major
V_7 chord = G B D F

A dominant seventh (V_7) chord is merely a V chord plus ___7th___ .

Check your answer in part 289.

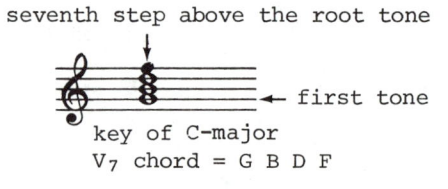

ANSWER: The seventh tone of that chord

Diagnostic Question Five

At the beginning of this chapter, a CADENCE was defined as a series of chords that conveys the impression of conclusion. Cadences are found at the end of phrases, sections of music, or complete pieces. Three of the more common cadential patterns are given below. Match the two columns and choose the correct alternative.

C 1. plagal or amen cadence   A. progression from V to I
A 2. authentic cadence   B. progression from IV to V to I
B 3. mixed cadence   C. progression from IV to I

Alternatives

		part
a.	Rather than guess, I would like to read the explanation.	291
(b.)	1 = C 2 = A 3 = B	290
c.	1 = A 2 = C 3 = B	284

290

Excellent. The authentic cadence (V-I) is the most common cadence. The plagal cadence is sometimes called the amen cadence because the word amen is sung at the end of hymns on the chords IV-I (a-men). When the authentic and plagal cadences are combined, a mixed cadence (IV-V-I) is formed.

Now look at the song "American the Beautiful" (part 251). What kind of cadence does it have at the end of the song? (To answer the question, determine the notes of the last chord in the song. It should be the I chord. Then determine the notes of the next-to-last chord and see what cadence results.) To check your answer turn to part 292.

291

ABOUT CADENCES: The most common cadence involves the two strongest chords in any key: the V and the I (or the V_7 and I). It is called an AUTHENTIC cadence.

Another common cadence involves the IV and I chords. It is called the PLAGAL or AMEN cadence. The word AMEN is used in this description because the cadence is used at the conclusion of so many religious hymns as follows:

                  hymn text: a-men
            plagal cadence: IV-I

Obviously, the authentic and plagal cadences can be combined. When MIXED, the IV chord usually precedes the V chord: IV-V-I.

To review the three cadences:

        V-I: authentic cadence (most common)
        IV-I: plagal or amen cadence
        IV-V-I: mixed cadence

Return to the Diagnostic Question in part 289.

ANSWER: "America the Beautiful" ends with an authentic cadence.

Congratulations, you have now completed chapter 5 of the program. The following Proficiency Developers will help you develop skills relating to the concepts just learned. Do each of the suggested activities until you feel comfortable with the process.

Proficiency Developers

1. Sing the song "A Frog Went A-Courting," first using words, then sol-fa syllables, and finally tone numbers for the scale degree represented by each note. You may have to sing the song at a slower tempo in order to do it right the first few times. Then sing other songs in the book using the same process.

A FROG WENT A-COURTING

English Folk Song

Turn to part 293.

293

[Music notation: Eb, Ab, Eb, Ab, Eb chords; lyrics: "by his side, uh-huh! uh-huh! uh-huh!"]

2: He rode up to Miss Mousie's door, uh-huh
   He rode up to Miss Mousie's door, uh-huh
   He rode up to Miss Mousie's door
   With his coat all buttoned down before, uh-huh, uh-huh, uh-huh.

3: He took Miss Mousie on his knee, uh-huh
   He took Miss Mousie on his knee, uh-huh
   He took Miss Mousie on his knee
   And said "My dear, will you marry me?" uh-huh, uh-huh, uh-huh.

4: Oh no, kind sir, I can't say that, uh-huh
   Oh no, kind sir, I can't say that, uh-huh
   Oh no, kind sir, I can't say that
   You'll have to ask my Uncle Rat, uh-huh, uh-huh, uh-huh.

5: Uncle Rat, he laughed and shook his fat side, uh-huh
   Uncle Rat, he laughed and shook his fat side, uh-huh
   Uncle Rat, he laughed and shook his fat side
   To think that his niece would be a bride, uh-huh, uh-huh, uh-huh.

6: Oh, where shall the wedding breakfast be, uh-huh
   Oh, where shall the wedding breakfast be, uh-huh
   Oh, where shall the wedding breakfast be
   Way down in the woods in a hollow tree, uh-huh, uh-huh, uh-huh.

2. Play "A Frog Went A-Courting" on the piano, or on some other instrument until you can play it without interruption.

3. Improvise a harmony line to the melody of "A Frog Went A-Courting" and write your harmonization on the staff with the melody. (You should find yourself using many thirds and sixths.)

Turn to part 294.

294

4. "The Muffin Man" is written below in the key of G. On the blank staff lines following the song, transpose the song to the key of F-major. To transpose, think of each note, not by note name, but by its sol-fa syllable or by its assigned number, 1-8, in the scale. Then write the note in the key of F bearing the same syllable or number.

MUFFIN MAN

O, do you know the Muf - fin Man, the
Muf - fin Man, the Muf - fin Man? O, do you know the
Muf - fin Man, who lives in Dru - ry lane?

```
2: Oh, yes I know the Muffin Man. . . .
3: Have you seen the Muffin Man? . . .
4: Oh, yes I've seen the Muffin Man. . . .
5: Do you like the Muffin Man? . . .
6: Oh, yes I like the Muffin Man. . . .
```

O, do you know the Muf - fin Man, the
Muf - fin Man, the Muf - fin Man? O, do you know the
Muf - fin Man, who lives in Dru - ry lane?

Turn to part 295.

5. Identify the chords needed to harmonize "Muffin Man" and write the chord name above the appropriate measure. You will need the I, ii (as a substitute for the IV) or the IV, and the V chords.
6. Look up any five songs in the book. What cadences do they employ at their conclusion? Is one used more frequently than others?

« Just for Fun »

Here are several "fun songs" that can make any classroom more enjoyable. Try them yourself and use them when appropriate.

THIS POOR OLD SLAVE

This poor old slave is gone to rest, he knows he now is free. His bones they lie (disturb them not) way down in Ten-nes-see.

1: Sing it as it is.
2: End the second phrase with "free-o-free-free," and phrase four with "Tennes-see-o-see." The rest is unchanged.
3: Repeat the first word of each measure rapidly (e.g., poor-poor, slave-slave, gone-gone). The rest of the song is sung like verse 2.
4: On the first word of each measure, sing the opening consonant, then "ee," followed by the rest of the word. For example, "This pee-or old slee-ave is gee-one to ree-st," etc.
5: On the first word of each measure sing the opening consonant followed by the sound "iggidy," then the complete word. For example, "This piggidy-poor old sliggidy-slave is giggidy-gone to riggidy-rest."

Turn to part 296.

296

Sing the round "Are You Sleeping, Brother John." Then sing the Hawaiian version of it found below.

LILI OU KALANI

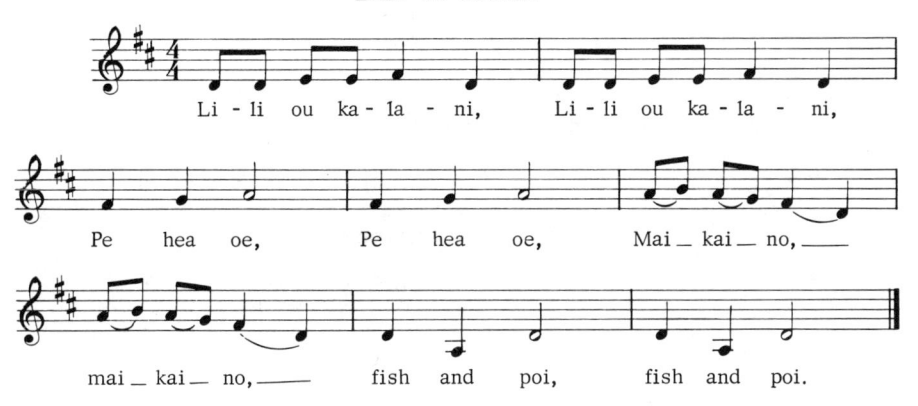

Li - li ou ka - la - ni, Li - li ou ka - la - ni,
Pe hea oe, Pe hea oe, Mai kai no,
mai kai no, fish and poi, fish and poi.

Turn to the song "Bingo" (part 46). Sing it as it is the first time. Each subsequent time omit one more letter from the spelling of B - I - N - G - O, and clap in its place. (For example, the third time will be "clap-clap-clap-G-O." Continue until all letters are omitted.

Turn to the song "Little Tom Tinker" (part 109). Sing it as a round, repeating it three times. Separate the class into groups. The first time have each group throw their hands in the air twice as they sing the words "ma—, ma—." The second time have them stand up twice quickly while singing the same words, and the last time have them combine both previous actions. When done as a round, it can be very comical.

Turn to part 297.

297

Self-Test

You are now ready to evaluate your understanding of the material in this chapter so you can determine which concepts you should review.

Listed below are five terms and five definitions. Write the letter of the correct definition by each term.

1. key _C_

   A. a series of chords that conveys the impression of conclusion

2. cadence _A_

   B. a series of tones in ascending or descending order, beginning with the key tone, and maintaining fixed distances between all tones

3. tonality _D_

   C. any group of tones that are drawn to a central tone, and bear its name

4. key tone _E_

   D. the organization of tones around a key tone—the tendency to return to a key tone for the feeling of conclusion

5. scale _B_

   E. the central tone to which other tones are drawn—where complete repose is found

Shown below is an example of the G-major scale. Under certain notes are numbers and blanks. Use each blank to write the number of the note directly above it, indicating the note's position in relation to the rest of the notes in the scale.

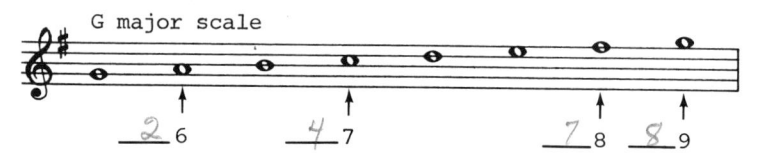

G major scale

_2_ 6   _4_ 7   _7_ 8 _8_ 9

10. _3/4_   In any major scale, the notes are all whole steps apart except for two places, where the notes are only half steps apart. Write the numbers of the notes between

11. _7/8_   which the half steps exist in blanks 10 and 11.

Turn to part 298.

12. Below, the scale is represented by the numbers 1 through 8. Draw an arrow from note 7 to its note of resolution. Then do the same for notes 2 and 5.

1 2 3 4 5 6 7 8

13. Look at the final cadence in "A Frog Went A-Courting" (part 292). What name do we give cadences that employ these chords? *plagal*

14. Are any chords employed in "A Frog Went A-Courting" not primary triads? If so, what chords are they, and where are they located? *None*

In the tonic sol-fa system each note of the scale has a syllable. Write the correct syllable under each specified note of the A-major scale below.

Do 15   *Mi* 16   *Sol* 17   *Ti* 18   *Do* 19

Identify each of the following key signatures.

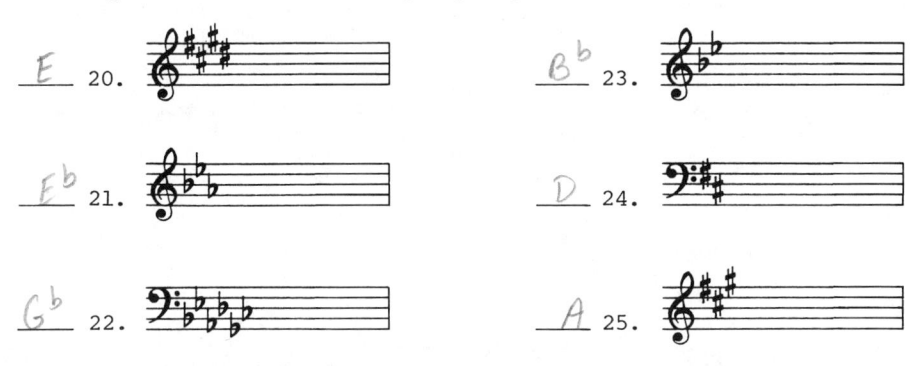

E 20.

E♭ 21.

G♭ 22.

B♭ 23.

D 24.

A 25.

Go to part 299.

26. _C#_ to _D_   In the key of A-major, the half steps fall
                 between which notes? (Write your answers by
27. _G#_ to _A_ numbers 26 and 27.)
28. _D_ to _Eb_ Where will they fall in the key of B-flat
                 major? (Write your answers in blanks 28 and
29. _A_ to _Bb_ 29.)

On the staff below is the B-flat major scale with chords built on each scale tone. Each of these chords has a name. Write the chord name under the chords that are indicated.

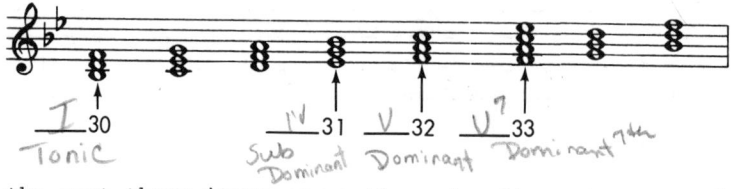

_I_ 30   _IV_ 31   _V_ 32   _V7_ 33
Tonic   Sub   Dominant Dominant 7th
          Dominant

Match the next three items correctly and write your answer in the blank at the left.

34. tonic chord _B_   A. the second most important
                                 chord in the key—the primary
                                 chord of departure

35. subdominant chord _C_   B. the fundamental chord of any
                                 key, toward which all other
                                 chords in the key lead

36. dominant chord _A_   C. the third most important chord
                                 in any key

37. _vi_ Which chord may be substituted for the I chord?
38. _ii_ For the IV chord?
39. _iii_ For the V chord?
40. _D_   In the example at the right
          is the V chord in the key
          of A-major. To make it a
          V7 chord what note would
          you add?

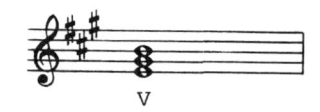

                                                    V

Turn to part 300.

300

41. __V I__ Write the roman numerals that indicate the chord progression used in the AUTHENTIC cadence.

42. __IV I__ Write the roman numerals that indicate the chord progression of the PLAGAL (AMEN) cadence.

43. __IV V I__ Write the roman numerals that indicate the chord progression of the MIXED cadence.

Determine the names of the following three mystery tunes by translating the sol-fa system into real pitches. The rhythm is not precisely notated, but the measures are marked with slashes, and arrows indicate whether some pitches are below or above the preceding pitches.

44. __This Old Man__
45. __London Bridge__
46. __Farmer in the Dell__

    (44) sol ↓ mi ↑ sol—/ sol mi sol—/ la sol fa mi/ re mi fa mi fa/ sol do do

    (45) sol la sol fa / mi fa sol—/ re mi fa—/ mi fa sol—/ sol la sol fa/

    (46) sol/ ↑ do do do do do re/ mi mi mi mi mi/ ↑ sol sol la sol mi do re/

47. In the blank space below, complete these 7 steps:
    a. Draw the five lines of the staff across the entire page.
    b. Put the bass clef sign on the staff.
    c. Write in the key signature for B♭-major.
    d. Write in the notes of the B♭-major scale on the staff.
    e. Write in the notes of the I, IV, and V chords.
    f. Make a V$_7$ chord out of the V chord by adding the appropriate note.
    g. Write the names of the chords under notes 1, 4, and 5.

Now turn to the answer key in part 301.

Please check your answers with those in the key that follows. Be sure to review each missed question by looking up the topic in parenthesis. If you missed a substantial number of the questions you should review the entire chapter before going on.

Answers & Review Index

1. C (key defined 258)
2. A (cadence defined 258)
3. D (tonality defined 258)
4. E (key tone defined 258)
5. B (scale defined 258)
6. 2 (scale tone numbers 261)
7. 4 (scale tone numbers 261)
8. 7 (scale tone numbers 261)
9. 8 or 1 (scale tone numbers 261)
10. 3-4 (major scale half steps 258)
11. 7-8 (major scale half steps 258)
12. 1⌢2 3 4 5 6 7⌢8 (resolution of scale tones 282)
13. plagal cadence (cadences 291)
14. No, they are all primary chords; I, IV, V (primary chords 263)
15. do (sol-fa system 267)
16. mi (sol-fa system 267)
17. sol (sol-fa system 267)
18. ti (sol-fa system 267)
19. do (sol-fa system 267)
20. E-major (key signatures 268 ff)
21. E-flat major (key signatures 268 ff)
22. G-flat major (key signatures 268 ff)
23. B-flat major (key signatures 268 ff)
24. D-major (key signatures 268 ff)
25. A-major (key signatures 268 ff)
26. C-sharp-D (major scale half steps 258)
27. G-sharp-A (major scale half steps 258)
28. D-E-flat (major scale half steps 258)
29. A-B-flat (major scale half steps 258)
30. tonic (chord names 275)
31. subdominant (chord names 275)
32. dominant (chord names 275)
33. dominant seventh (288)
34. B (tonic chord 275)
35. C (subdominant chord 275)
36. A (dominant chord 275)
37. vi (substitute for I chord 263)
38. ii (substitute for IV chord 263)
39. iii (substitute for V chord 263)
40. D (V_7 chord 288)
41. V-I (authentic cadence 291)
42. IV-I (plagal cadence 291)

43. IV-V-I (mixed cadence 291)
44. "This Old Man" (sol-fa system 267)
45. "London Bridge" (sol-fa system 267)
46. "Farmer in the Dell" (sol-fa system 267)

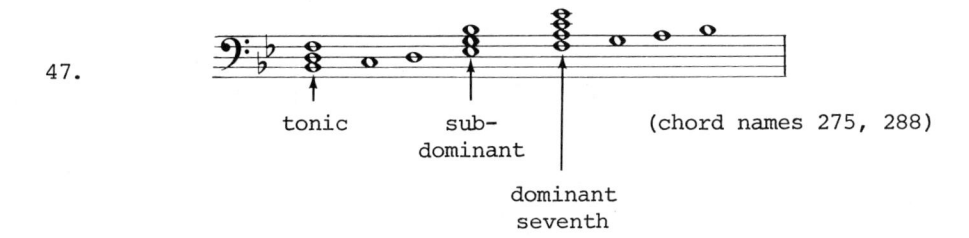

47.

    tonic   sub-   (chord names 275, 288)
            dominant
                    dominant
                    seventh

6
Minor Scales, Chords, and Keys

302

Although much of the material in the previous chapter pertains to minor, as well as major, scales and keys, there has been no discussion of minor keys and scales as such. The minor keys do much to enhance the sounds of music by bringing greater contrast—or another dimension—to the listener's ear. Whereas there is only one kind of major scale, there are three kinds of minor scales. The emphasis in this chapter will be on identifying minor keys, scales, and chords and their unique characteristics.

Objectives

1. Recall two ways major scales are like their relative minor scales, and two ways they are different.

2. Locate the relative minor scale for any major scale, and specify its key signature.

3. Differentiate between a NATURAL minor scale and a HARMONIC minor scale visually and verbally.

4. Recall the construction of minor triads, and how they differ from major triads.

5. Employ the minor circle of fifths to ascertain minor key signatures.

6. Identify the tones and the primary chords of the natural minor keys of C, A, and D.

7. Identify the tones and primary chords of the harmonic minor keys of C, A, and D.

There are four Diagnostic Questions in this chapter.

Go to part 303.

Let's analyze these two scales and see what similarities and differences exist.

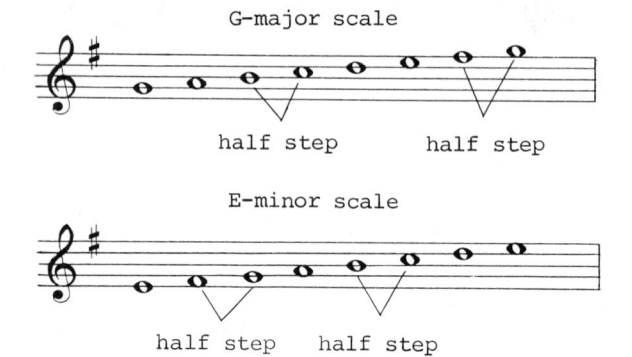

G-major scale

half step   half step

E-minor scale

half step   half step

SIMILARITIES

1. They have the same key signature: one sharp. When a major and minor scale have the same key signature they are called RELATIVE keys.

2. They both have notes on every line and space—no gaps.

DIFFERENCES

1. They start on different notes. Very important: THE RELATIVE MINOR SCALE STARTS A MINOR THIRD LOWER THAN THE MAJOR SCALE. Thus, in the example above, the G-major scale begins on G, and its relative minor scale on E.

2. The half steps do not occur in the same places:
   major scale: half steps between notes 3-4 and 7-8.
   minor scale: half steps between notes 2-3 and 5-6.
   As you can see, the half steps occur one step lower in the minor scale.

THREE PRINCIPLES

1. If a minor scale has the *same key signature* as a major scale, they are RELATIVE scales.

2. If a minor scale employs only the key signature of its relative major, i.e., no other tones of the scale are consistently altered, it is called a NATURAL minor scale.

3. Every major scale has a relative minor scale that uses the same key signature, and begins a MINOR THIRD LOWER.

Go to part 304.

304

Diagnostic Question One

On the left are names of three major scales. On the right are three minor scales. Choose the RELATIVE MINOR SCALE for each of the major scales.

Major Scales		Minor Scales
F-major	*D minor*	A-minor
C-major	*A minor*	G-minor
B♭-major	*G minor*	D-minor

Alternatives

		part
a.	I'm note sure. Please explain how to find relative keys.	325
(b.)	F-major and D-minor C-major and A-minor B♭-major and G-minor	306
c.	F-major and A-minor C-major and G-minor B♭-major and D-minor	314
d.	F-major and G-minor C-major and D-minor B♭-major and A-minor	309

305

Absolutely right. You seem to understand the construction of chords in the harmonic minor. Do these next few exercises.

C-minor scale (harmonic minor)

Use the Shield

In the above example (key of C-minor), the i chord will consist of which notes?

C, E-flat, and G   (Be sure to watch for the flats.)

In the same example, the iv chord will consist of which notes?

F, A-flat and C

The V chord will consist of which notes?

G, B, and D   (Remember the leading tone of the harmonic minor is only one half step from the tonic. This explains the B-natural above, and the major quality of the V chord.)

Put the Shield Aside

In chapter 5, the tonic sol-fa system was presented for the major scale as shown on the left.

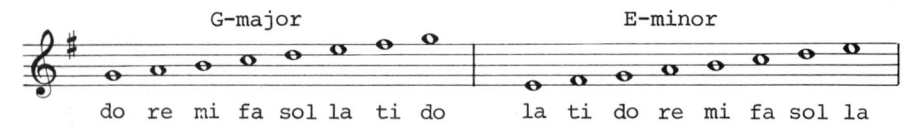

G-major   E-minor

do re mi fa sol la ti do   la ti do re mi fa sol la

For the natural minor scale, the sol-fa syllables begin and end with la, as illustrated on the right. This puts all half steps in their correct places for the minor scale. The tonic note of the minor scale will always bear the syllable la.

Go to part 326.

306

Correct. You have picked the relative minor scales for three major scales. Now examine the C natural minor scale and some of its characteristics.

QUESTION: What is the key signature for the key of C-minor?

ANSWER: Three flats: B♭, E♭, A♭. (The same as its relative major scale; E♭-major.)

Here are the C-major and C-minor scales. What differences do you see?

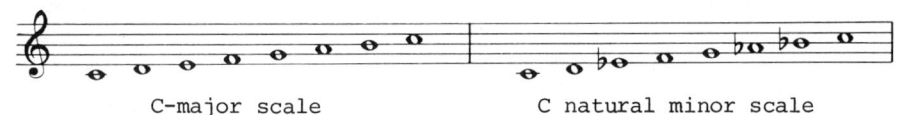

[musical notation: C-major scale | C natural minor scale]

DIFFERENCES

1. Compared to the C-major scale, the C-minor scale has lowered steps 3, 6, and 7.
2. The half steps fall between 2-3 and 5-6 in the minor scale.

IF YOU COMPARE ANY MAJOR SCALE WITH THE MINOR SCALE BEGINNING ON THE SAME NOTE, THESE DIFFERENCES WILL EXIST.

Use the Shield

When comparing major scales with natural minor scales, what notes are changed, and how?

Notes 3, 6, and 7 are lowered one half step.

The notes of the G-major scale are G A B C D E F♯ G. What are the notes of the G-minor scale?

G A B♭ C D E♭ F♮ G (notes 3, 6, 7 have been lowered)

Turn to part 308.

307

That wasn't quite right. Please read the information in part 319.

308

Use the Shield

The notes of the F-major scale are F G A B♭ C D E F. What are the notes of the F natural minor scale?

(handwritten above: A♭   D♭ E♭)

❧

F G A♭ B♭ C D♭ E♭ F   *(Notes 3, 6, 7 have been lowered.)*

The notes of the A-major scale are A B C♯ D E F♯ G♯ A. What are the notes of the A natural minor scale?

(handwritten above: C♮   F♮ G♮)

❧

A B C D E F G A   *(Lowering notes 3, 6, 7 cancels the sharps.)*

What is the relative minor scale for A♭-major?

❧

F-minor   *(a minor third lower)*

What is the key signature for A-minor?

❧

The same as its relative major, C-major: no sharps or flats.

What natural minor scale has the same key signature as F-major?

❧

D-minor   *(one flat: B♭)*

Go to part 310.

309

That wasn't quite right. Please read the information in part 325.

310

The key signatures for minor scales can also be determined by using a circle of fifths. Comparison of this circle of fifths to the circle in part 268 will show the differences between major and minor key signatures.

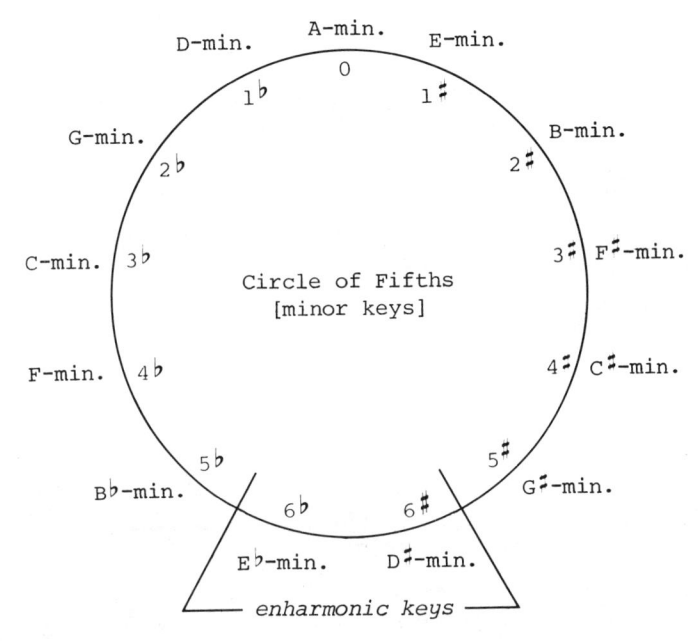

```
                    A-min.
        D-min.        0       E-min.
                 1♭       1♯
   G-min.                         B-min.
            2♭             2♯

C-min.   3♭                    3♯   F♯-min.
              Circle of Fifths
                [minor keys]

F-min.   4♭                    4♯   C♯-min.

            5♭             5♯
   B♭-min.                        G♯-min.
                 6♭       6♯
           E♭-min.    D♯-min.
              — enharmonic keys —
```

SUPPORTIVE SKILL: In any key signature using sharps, the sharps always appear in the same order as for major scales, namely: F♯, C♯, G♯, D♯, A♯, E♯. In any key signature involving flats, the flats always appear in the same order: B♭, E♭, A♭, D♭, G♭, C♭.

If a key signature uses three or four sharps or flats, they will be in the order listed above.

Go on to part 311.

311

Diagnostic Question Two

The primary chords in any key are the I, IV, and V chords. What happens to these chords in the natural minor scale?

Alternatives

		part
1.	I'm not sure, and I don't want to guess.	319
2.	The primary chords remain major chords in the natural minor scale.	307
3.	The primary chords all become minor chords in the natural minor scale.	316
4.	The primary chords cease to exist as primary chords in the natural minor scale.	317

312

The explanation is very simple. There is only one difference between the natural minor scale and the harmonic minor scale:

THE SEVENTH STEP OF THE SCALE IS RAISED ONE HALF STEP.

In this way the harmonic scale is like the MAJOR scale, isn't it? By raising it, it is now just one half step away from do. Now return to part 315.

313

Well, you seem to be confused about something. The review that will help you is in part 322.

314

That was an incorrect alternative. Please read the information in part 325.

We have explored the natural minor scale, its key signature, its primary triads, and its relationship to major scales. It is now time to turn our attention to another minor scale, the HARMONIC MINOR SCALE.

Diagnostic Question Three

How does the HARMONIC minor scale differ from the NATURAL minor scale?

Alternatives

		part
1.	I don't know. How about an explanation?	312
2.	The third, sixth, and seventh steps of the natural minor are lowered to create the harmonic minor.	318
3.	The harmonic minor begins on the note found a minor third below the first note of the natural minor scale.	323
4.	The seventh step of the natural minor is raised to make the harmonic minor.	320

316

That is right. The primary chords in the natural minor scale are all minor chords, designated by roman numerals i, iv, and v. The reason is easy to see. On the top staff below is the D-major scale; the black notes will be lowered to creat the minor scale. On the bottom staff is the D-minor scale, with the primary triads constructed on notes 1, 4, and 5. Notice that the middle note in each triad is lowered, making the bottom third minor, and thereby changing that triad from major to minor.

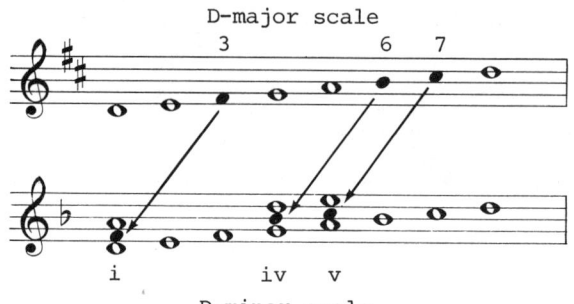

NOTE: Those three notes were lowered automatically when the major key signature of two sharps was changed to the minor key signature of one flat.

Go to part 315.

317

That wasn't quite right. Please read the information in part 319.

318

I'm sorry. That was not the correct alternative. Please turn to part 312.

319

The primary chords in major keys are major chords, designated by the roman numerals I, IV, and V. In the natural minor scale, the primary chords all become minor chords, designated by the roman numerals i, iv, and v. Return to part 311.

320

You are right. The harmonic minor differs from the natural minor in one simple way: THE SEVENTH STEP IS RAISED ONE HALF STEP.

That's a simple change, but it involves several interesting ramifications:

1. The reason the seventh step is raised is to keep it one half step away from do, thus preserving its strong tendencies as the leading tone to do. The distance between the seventh and eighth steps (one half step) is the same as it is in the major scale.

2. This change in the seventh step does not take place in the key signature. It is raised on the staff every time it appears by adding the proper ACCIDENTAL (a sharp, flat, or natural sign).

3. In the natural minor scale, the primary triads are all minor. When the seventh step is raised in the harmonic minor, the resulting V chord is MAJOR. THE PRINCIPLE TRIADS OF THE HARMONIC MINOR ARE i, iv, AND V.

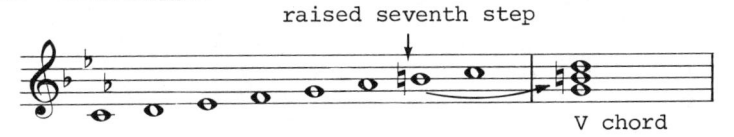

Turn to part 321.

Diagnostic Question Four

Carefully select the correct response below.

Which of the following alternatives correctly identifies the i, iv, and V chords in the key of A harmonic minor?

Alternatives

		part
a.	I don't quite understand. Please direct me to an explanation.	322
b.	i chord = A C E iv chord = D F A V chord = E G B	324
c.	i chord = A C♯ E iv chord = D F♯ A V chord = E G♯ B	313
d.	i chord = A C E iv chord = D F A V chord = E G♯ B	305

322

A-minor scale

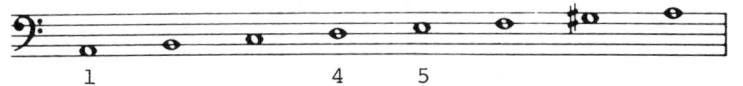

[Bass clef staff showing A-minor scale with notes marked 1, 4, 5]

In the question you were asked to identify the notes of the i, iv, and V chords in A-minor. In the example above, notes 1, 4, and 5, which will form the respective roots of the three triads, are identified.

Triads

  i = note A and the two spaces above A, namely, C and E
 iv = note D and the two lines above D, namely, F and A
  V = note E and the two spaces above E, namely, G♯ and B
      (The G is sharped because it is the seventh step of
      the harmonic minor scale.)

$$\text{i is a minor triad}$$
$$\text{iv is a minor triad}$$
$$\text{V is a major triad}$$

Return to part 321.

323

I'm sorry. That was not the correct alternative. Please turn to part 312.

324

That wasn't correct. Please go to part 322 for an explanation.

325

It may seem confusing now, but it will become easy to locate relative minor keys. Assume, for example, that we have a major scale beginning on the note E♭. The rule quoted earlier said that the relative minor scale always begins on the note a MINOR THIRD LOWER.

1. Find the note a THIRD lower. The next lower line in this example is middle C.

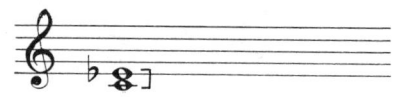

    one third lower

2. Determine whether the third is of major or minor quality. Assuming that the bottom note (C) is the first note of the C-major scale, we discover that the E♭ is NOT in that major scale. Hence, the third (C to E♭) is minor.

3. Having found the note a minor third below, we have learned that C-minor is the relative minor of E♭-major.

Now try this example: What is the relative minor scale of G-major? (Use the staff below to figure out your answer.)

1. What note is a third lower than G?

2. Is that third of major or minor quality?

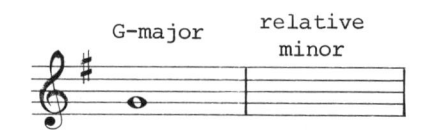

    G-major   relative minor

3. If it is a minor third, the scale beginning on that note is the relative minor scale. If it is a major third, raise your bottom note one half step so it becomes a minor third, and THAT NOTE is the relative minor.

Now return to the Diagnostic Question in part 304 and apply the rule. (By the way, the answer to the above question is E-minor.)

326

If you go down from <u>do</u> to <u>la</u>, you have dropped a minor third, the same distance you drop to find the relative minor scale for any major one.

IN MINOR SCALES, THE HOME TONE IS DESIGNATED <u>LA</u>, WITH THE SYLLABLES THEN FOLLOWING IN NORMAL ORDER.

You have just finished chapter 6. In order to increase your competency with the concepts discussed, please do all the Proficiency Developers below.

Proficiency Developers

1. On the staff lines below, complete the following steps:

    a. Put the treble clef sign of the staff.
    b. Write in the key signature for D-minor.
    c. Write the notes of the D natural minor scale.
    d. Write in the notes of the tonic, subdominant, and dominant chords.
    e. Designate them as major or minor triads using upper- or lower-case roman numerals.

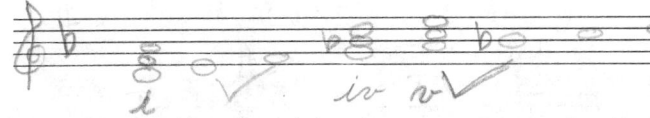

2. What is the relative minor key for each of these major keys?

    F-major = D minor   G-major = E minor
    B♭-major = G minor   C-major = A minor

3. Sing "Who Has Seen the Wind" (part 327) with words, then with sol-fa syllables, using the minor names introduced in part 305.

Turn to part 327, please.

327

WHO HAS SEEN THE WIND?*

Christina Rosetti Edmund F. Soule

Continued on the following page.

*Used with permission, Edmund F. Soule, University of Oregon, Eugene, Oregon.

Please continue to part 328.

328

4. Sing "When Johnny Comes Marching Home" with words. Then sing it again with sol-fa syllables, using the minor names introduced in part 305.

WHEN JOHNNY COMES MARCHING HOME

Anonymous
Civil War Song

When John-ny comes march-ing home a-gain, hur-rah! hur-rah! We'll give him a heart-y wel-come then, hur-rah, hur-rah! The men will cheer, the boys will shout, the la-dies, they will all turn out, and we'll all feel gay when John-ny comes march-ing home!

Turn to part 329.

Verse

2. The old church bells will peal for joy, Hurrah, Hurrah!
   To welcome home our darling boy, Hurrah, Hurrah!
   The village lads and lasses gay,
   With roses they will strew the way,
   And we'll all feel gay when Johnny comes marching home.

3. Get ready for the jubilee, Hurrah, Hurrah!
   We'll give the heroes "three times three," Hurrah, Hurrah!
   The laurel wreath is ready now
   To place upon his loyal brow,
   And we'll all feel gay when Johnny comes marching home!

5. The chords for "When Johnny Comes Marching Home" are indicated above the staff. Write the notes of each chord on the empty bass clef staff, putting one chord in every measure.

6. "The Farmer in the Dell" (in G-major) is found in part 108. Rewrite it below in the key of G-minor. Then play it and sing it several times to get used to the new sound of its melody.

FARMER IN THE DELL

The far - mer in the dell, the far - mer in the dell,

heigh - ho, the derry - o, the far - mer in the dell.

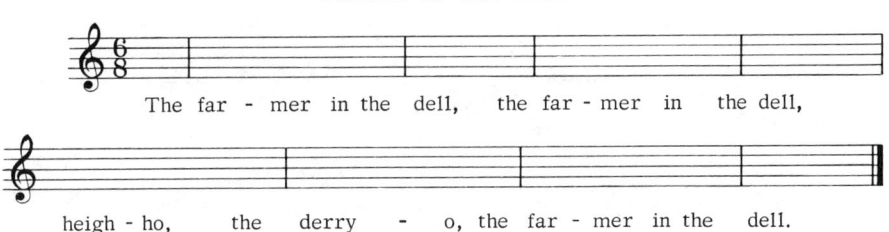

Now turn to part 330.

330

« Just for Fun »

Don't take the Self-Test until you have tried to correct these misspelled words. (How many can you get right?)

KOREKTENG BADD SPELING INN MUSICK WORRDES*

Listed below are some musical terms that are most often misspelled. Next to the word, write its correct spelling.

1. ukelele _____
2. accedentels _____
3. saxaphone _____
4. retard _____
5. accapella _____
6. acordian _____
7. acompanyment _____
8. coronet _____
   (brass instrument)
9. cannon _____
   (round)
10. chior _____

11. picallo _____
12. cleff _____
13. simbal _____
14. clarionet _____
15. fiddel _____
16. marracas _____
17. fluet _____
18. tamberene _____
19. rithem _____
20. base vile _____

These "badd spelings" weren't just made up—they were taken from students who knew what they meant but couldn't spell them on tests, papers, reports, and so on. Of course, we know that they meant, but it helps to be literate in our own written language. You can check your spelling accuracy in part 333.

Please continue to part 331.

*Used with permission, Karen Kammerer, University of Oregon, Eugene, Oregon.

331

Self-Test

Mark the following statements with T for true or F for false.

1. _F_ Steps 3 to 4 and 7 to 8 are half steps in the minor scale.
2. _T_ There are several kinds of minor scales.
3. _T_ The I, IV, and V chords of the major key become minor chords in the natural minor key.
4. _T_ Steps 2 to 3 and 5 to 6 are half steps in the minor scale.
5. _F_ The fourth and fifth tones of the major scale are lowered in the minor scale.
6. _T_ The fourth and fifth tones of the major scale remain the same in the minor scale.
7. _T_ A minor triad has a minor third for its bottom interval.
8. _T_ The third and sixth tones of the major scale are lowered in the harmonic minor.
9. _T_ Every major scale has a relative minor scale.
10. _F_ The only difference between the natural minor and the harmonic minor scales is that the third tone of the harmonic minor is one half step lower.
11. _T_ In the natural minor scale, steps 3, 6, and 7 have been lowered from the major scale.

Answer the following questions:

12. _____ Is the melody of "When Johnny Comes Marching Home" in the natural or harmonic minor?
13. _____ In which minor scale are the primary triads i, iv, and V? (natural or harmonic minor)

Continued in part 332.

332

Identify each of the MINOR keys represented by the three key signatures that follow.

14. _D minor_

15. _B♭ minor_

16. _F# minor_

17. _Key Sig._ Relative keys (i.e., relative major or minor keys) are two keys that have the same _____ _____ .

18. _E m_ What is the relative minor of G-major?

19. _B♭ M_ What is the relative major of G-minor?

20. _D F A_ In the D-harmonic minor scale, the i chord will contain which three notes?

21. _G B♭ D_ In the D-harmonic minor scale, the iv chord will contain which three notes?

22. _A C# E_ In this scale, which three notes will the V chord contain?

23. _½ step_ An important characteristic of the leading tone is that it is only (how far) from the tonic in the harmonic minor?

24. _3_ The note G on this staff is on what scale step of the minor key represented by the key signature?

25. _i_ What chord is this in the minor key represented by the key signature?

Now that you have completed the test, turn to part 333 for the Answers and Review Index. After reviewing every question you missed, proceed to chapter 7. If you missed numerous answers, you should probably reread chapter 6.

Turn the page for part 333.

Answers & Review Index

1. F (half steps in minor scales 303, 306)
2. T (different kinds of minor scales 312)
3. T (chords of minor keys 316)
4. T (half steps in minor keys 303)
5. F (characteristics of minor scales 303 ff, 306)
6. T (characteristics of minor scales 303 ff, 306)
7. T (minor triads 316)
8. T (characteristics of harmonic minor scales 312)
9. T (relative major and minor keys 325)
10. F (characteristics of the harmonic minor 312)
11. T (characteristics of the natural minor 303 ff, 306)
12. natural (characteristics of the harmonic minor 320)
13. harmonic (harmonic minor chords 320)
14. D-minor (minor key signatures 310)
15. B-flat minor (minor key signatures 310)
16. F-sharp minor (minor key signatures 310)
17. key signature (relative major and minor keys 325 ff)
18. E-minor (relative major and minor keys 325 ff)
19. B♭-major (relative major and minor keys 325 ff)
20. D-F-A (chords in minor keys 315)
21. G-B♭-D (chords in minor keys 315)
22. A-C♯-E (chords in minor keys 315)
23. one half step (harmonic minor scale 312)
24. third (minor key signatures 310)
25. i chord (chords in minor keys 310, 316)

KOREKTENG BADD SPELING INN MUSICK WORRDES

1. ukulele
2. accidentals
3. saxophone
4. ritard
5. acappella
6. accordian
7. accompaniment
8. cornet
9. canon
10. choir
11. piccolo
12. clef
13. cymbal
14. clarinet
15. fiddle
16. maracas
17. flute
18. tambourine
19. rhythm
20. bass viol

7
The Structure of Music

=========== 334 ===========

In the same way that we can examine the tools, equipment, and raw materials used in the construction of a house, we have examined many of the materials used in the construction of music. It is now necessary to examine briefly how these materials can be put together, i.e., how a musical structure is formed.

In this chapter, you will be working to accomplish the following:

Objectives

1. Recognize the definitions of phrase, motive, sequence, and period.
2. Identify phrases, motives, sequences, and periods in musical contexts.
3. Recognize definitions for each of the following terms: AB form, two-part song form, ABA form, three-part song form, binary, ternary, free form.
4. Identify several forms in musical contexts.
5. Describe the relationship between cadences and phrases.

Achievement of this chapter's objectives will help you become a more perceptive listener and furnish insight into the constructional procedures used in writing music. Moreover, it should increase your understanding of musical principles and your appreciation of the art form. Although it is beyond the scope of this book to deal at length with form in music, the rudimentary forms presented here will provide the basis for understanding other, more sophisticated forms.

There are three Diagnostic Questions in this chapter.

Turn to part 335.

Diagnostic Question One

On the left are four terms that describe segments of music. See if you can correctly match them with the definitions on the right.

1. phrase
2. sequence
3. period
4. motive

A. a series of notes that leads to, and reaches, a place of resolution or repose

B. a brief musical idea or gesture of a few notes length

C. a combination of two or more phrases

D. a musical fragment repeated several times, each time at a different pitch level

Alternatives

		part
a.	I would only be guessing if I matched them. Where is the explanation?	336
b.	1 = B 2 = D 3 = A 4 = C	345
c.	1 = A 2 = D 3 = C 4 = B	352
d.	1 = D 2 = A 3 = B 4 = C	339

The smallest unit in music, called a MOTIVE, is a short musical idea or a gesture. It is usually only a few notes in length. In "Polly Wolly Doodle," the chorus begins with a motive:

[musical notation: "Fare thee well, fare thee well" with two motives marked]

The term PHRASE is the most commonly mentioned unit in music. A phrase is a series of notes that progresses to a point of resolution, or repose. In other words, it is the PROGRESSION OF NOTES FROM ONE CADENCE TO ANOTHER. An example (from "Oh Susanna") with two phrases follows:

[musical notation: "I came from Alabama with my banjo on my knee, I'm goin' to Lou'siana my true love for to see." with two phrases marked]

Two phrases will frequently fit together as a unit to form a PERIOD, as illustrated in the example above. A period is the largest of the units considered here. In order of size from the smallest to largest, the units are: motive, phrase, period.

A SEQUENCE is a musical fragment that is repeated several times, each time at a different pitch level. You could make a sequence of five repetitions of the "Polly Wolly Doodle" motive above by treating it this way:

[musical notation: "fare thee well, fare thee well, fare thee well, fare thee well, fare thee well my fair-y fay,"]

Now return to part 335.

337

No, you made an error. The numbers enclosed a phrase, not a period. A brief review should clarify the matter. It is in part 349.

338

You have chosen the wrong alternative. Please read the analysis of the song in part 357.

339

You have made a mistake somewhere. Please go to part 336.

340

Let's examine the idea of phrases ending in cadences. In "Oh Susanna," the song starts on the tonic chord of the key (F), and progresses to the dominant-seventh (C_7) on the word "knee." That cadence (I-V_7) is a HALF-CADENCE, and marks the first place in the song where a feeling of repose is established. In this case, the repose is momentary because of the nature of the cadence. Phrases that end in half-cadences are frequently called ANTECEDENT phrases to signify the fleeting nature of the pause, and the concomitant expectation of something yet to come. Phrases ending with authentic or plagal cadences have a more stable feeling of conclusion, and are called CONSEQUENT phrases. The second, or consequent, phrase of "Oh Susanna" employs an authentic cadence, which establishes a more complete sense of repose at number 3.

OH SUSANNA

Stephen Foster

① F
I came from Al - a - bam - a with my ban - jo on my

C_7 ② F C_7
knee, I'm going to Loui - si - an - a, my true love for to

F ③
see. It rained all night the day I left, the weath - er it was

Continued in part 341.

341

dry, the sun so hot I froze to death, Su-san-na don't you cry. Oh Su-san-na, oh don't you cry for me, for I'm going to Loui-si-an-a with my ban-jo on my knee.

2. I had a dream the other night, when everything was still,
   I thought I saw Susanna a-coming down the hill.
   A buckwheat cake was in her mouth, a tear was in her eye,
   says I, "I'm coming from the south, Susanna don't you cry."
   CHORUS

Turn to part 342.

342

Diagnostic Question Two

Which of the following terms properly describes the part between ② and ③ in the song, "Oh Susanna" (parts 340, 341)?

Alternatives

		part
a.	I don't know. Could you please explain?	349
b.	phrase	344
c.	period	337
d.	motive	350

343

That is right. The song has ternary form (AABA). Listed below are several songs that employ the forms we have discussed. It would be beneficial for you to examine them to determine where the phrases are and why they are classified under that particular form.

Binary Form

"This Old Man," part 45
"Go Tell Aunt Rhody," part 46
"On Top of Old Smoky," part 353
"Polly Wolly Doodle" (verse) part 347

"Billy Boy," part 200
"Clementine"*
"Yankee Doodle" (verse), part 107
"Auld Lang Syne*

Ternary Form

"The More We get Together." part 355
"Twinkle, Twinkle Little Star"*
"Au Clair de la Lune," part 354

"Old MacDonald," part 49
"Alouette," part 199
"All Through the Night"*

Free Form

"America the Beautiful," part 251
"A Frog Went A-Courting," part 292

"When Johnny Comes Marching Home," part 328

Turn to part 358.

*These songs are not in this book, but are common examples of the form indicated.

344

Of course. The numbers enclosed the second phrase of the song, which ends with an authentic cadence (V-I).

Use the Shield

[musical notation: Twin-kle, twin-kle, lit-tle star, how I won-der what you are.]

What part of this song is enclosed in brackets? How does it end?

the first phrase, which ends with an authentic cadence

[musical notation: Oh I went down South for to see my gal, Sing Pol-ly Wol-ly doo-dle all the day.]

What part of the above song is enclosed in brackets?

a motive, which is repeated in the next five notes

Go to part 346.

345

You must have overlooked something. Please go to part 336.

346

SWING LOW SWEET CHARIOT
Spiritual

Swing low, sweet char-i-ot,— Com-ing for to car-ry me home! Swing low, sweet char-i-ot,— Com-ing for to car-ry me home! I looked o-ver Jor-dan and what did I see?— Com-ing for to car-ry me home! A band of an-gels com-ing aft-er me,— Com-ing for to car-ry me home.

2. If you get there before I do, coming for to carry me home,
   Tell all my friends I'll be there too, coming for to carry me home.

3. The brightest day that ever I saw, coming for to carry me home,
   When Jesus washed my sins away, coming for to carry me home.

4. I'm sometimes up and sometimes down, coming for to carry me home.
   But still my soul feels heavenly bound, coming for to carry me home.

Use this song to answer the questions that begin in part 347.

347

Use the Shield

What part of the song is found between numbers ① and ③ ?

☙

a period

Look at the same example. What term is used to describe the part of music between ① and ② ? How does the part end?

☙

a phrase (it ends with a half-cadence on V)

In that same example, do motives exist? If so, where?

☙

yes, measures 1-2 or 3-4 are examples of motives.

POLLY WOLLY DOODLE

Southern Folk Song

Oh I went down South for to see my Sal, Sing Pol-ly Wol-ly Doo-dle all the day, My Sal she am a spunk-y gal, Sing Pol-ly Wol-ly Doo-dle all the day! Fare thee well, fare thee well, fare thee well my fair-y fay! For I'm going to Loui-si-an-na, for to see my Su-sy-an-na, sing Pol-ly Wol-ly Dood-le all the day!

348

CHORUS

2: Oh my Sal, she is a maiden fair, etc.
   With laughing eyes and curly hair, etc.
   CHORUS
3: Behind the barn, upon my knees, etc.
   I thought I heard a chicken sneeze, etc.
   CHORUS
4: He sneezed so hard with whooping cough, etc.
   He sneezed his head and tail right off, etc.
   CHORUS
5: Oh a grasshopper sitting on a railroad track, etc.
   Just picking his teeth with a carpet tack, etc.
   CHORUS

The first phrase of "Polly Wolly Doodle" begins at number 1. On which number does the first phrase end? (See below)

☙

at number 4

Put the Shield Aside

Please turn to part 351.

349

Earlier in the program, a phrase was defined as a progression of notes leading to a place of repose, or resolution; a cadence was described as the place where the sense of repose is achieved. The song in the example was in the key of F-major. The unit you were to identify ended on the I chord (FAC) and was preceded by the V chord (CEG), thus creating an authentic cadence. The unit was too long to be a motive, nor could it be divided into two units, thereby making it a period. The unit is, therefore, a phrase. Phrases, incidentally, are frequently four measures long.

Now return to part 342.

350

No, you must have overlooked something. The letters enclosed a phrase, not a motive. Read the brief explanation in part 349.

351

Phrases of a song can be organized in many different ways to form different kinds of patterns.

Listed on the left are six patterns of music with a blank after each of them. On the right are three descriptions, lettered A through C. Write the proper letter after each of the terms on the left. (Some of the letters will be used more than once.)

1. binary _____
2. ABA _____
3. free _____
4. ternary _____
5. AB _____

A. A form frequently referred to as two-part song form. It consists of two main sections of music one of which may be repeated.

B. A song form that follows no set pattern and is not repeated.

C. This is a three-part song form. It involves the idea of establishing a melody, going to something new, and returning to the first melody at the conclusion.

After writing in your answers, turn to part 353 and grade them. Follow the instructions at the end of that part.

352

Absolutely right. Now we want to identify these terms in musical examples. For that, go to part 340.

353

Your answers in part 351 should read as follows:

1. (binary) A   4. (ternary) C
2. (ABA) C   5. (AB) A
3. (free) B

BINARY form consists of two different phrases (the prefix Bi-) in binary indicating two parts. If the first phrase is identified as A, the second phrase would be identified as B. Therefore, the form is also known as AB form. The form is also identified with a third name, TWO-PART FORM. An example of this form is found in the following song.

ON TOP OF OLD SMOKY

On top of Old Smok-y_____ all cov-ered with snow_____ I lost my true lov-er_____ come court-ing too slow._____

2. For courting's a pleasure, and parting is grief,
   But a false hearted lover is worse than a thief.

3. A thief will just rob you, and take what you have,
   But a false hearted lover will lead you to the grave.

4. They'll hug you and kiss you, and tell you more lies,
   Than ties on a railroad, or stars in the skies.

Turn to part 354.

354

In "On Top of Old Smoky," phrase ① begins the song and ends on the word "snow." Phrase ② starts with the word "I" and goes to the end. Any song that consists of two different phrases may be called two-part, or binary form.

The THREE PART or TERNARY song form is one of the most important forms in music and perhaps the most frequently used. The word "ternary" means divided into three parts.

The basis of ternary form is a fundamental principle of musical composition. This principle can be described with three words: establish, depart, and return; or with three letters: A, B, A. Using this form, a composer establishes a melody in the first part of the composition. At the beginning of the second part he leaves the established sound to introduce a new melody—part B. When this second part is completed, the music returns to the original melody, repeating the first phrase. The following diagram illustrates the ternary principle.

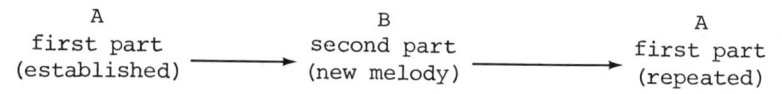

```
     A                    B                    A
first part    ──→    second part    ──→    first part
(established)        (new melody)           (repeated)
```

It should be mentioned that the first phrase of ternary song form is frequently repeated so the form actually is AABA; but the designation is usually abbreviated to ABA regardless of any repetition. A good example of this form is found in the following French folk song.

AU CLAIR DE LA LUNE
French Folk Song

Au clair de la lu - ne, mon a - mi Pier - rot,
Pre - te moi ta plu - me, pour e - crire un mot.
Ma chan - delle est mort - te, Je n'ai plus de feu,
Ou - vres moi ta por - te, pour l'a - mour de Dieu.

Turn to part 355.

In "Au Clair de la Lune," the first line is phrase A, and the second line is a repetition of the first. The third line begins a new melodic idea, and this is phrase B. The fourth line is once again a repetition of the first line, giving the song an AABA format, but still termed a ternary form.

Thus far we have discussed two forms: (1) binary or two-part form, and (2) ternary or three-part form. Another form, FREE FORM (occasionally referred to as "through composed," although this term is not technically correct), does not employ repetition. It may consist of any number of phrases, each one different from the former ones. If letters were assigned to each new phrase, the form would be ABCDE, etc., because of the lack of repetition of familiar material.

Diagnostic Question Three

Examine the song shown below and determine its form. Then select your alternative.

THE MORE WE GET TOGETHER

Alternatives

		part
a.	Please explain the answer.	257
b.	This song has binary form.	338
c.	This song has ternary form.	343
d.	This song has free form.	356

356

You chose the wrong alternative. Please read the information in part 357.

357

If you examine lines 1, 2, and 4 of the song (part 355), you will see that these musical lines are almost exactly the same. These phrases must, therefore, be labeled with the letter A.

     A   A   A

line 1   line 2   line 3   line 4

Only line 3 is different. It would, therefore, be identified as B. The form, then, is AABA, which is usually simplified to ABA, or ternary form.

Now return to part 355 and see if you can detect this form in the song.

358

The forms just discussed were all illustrated with relatively short folk tunes, but they have much wider application. Indeed, longer musical compositions performed by classical soloists, chamber ensembles, or full orchestras employ these same forms regularly. For example, binary form is utilized in much of the music written between 1600 and 1750 (e.g., the music of Bach and Handel). Part 359 is a well-known excerpt from Johann Sebastian Bach, "Orchestral Suite no. 3 in D-Major." The excerpt is titled "Air" and is in binary form. Parts A and B are marked by repeat signs: ‖:A:‖ ‖:B:‖.

Go to part 359.

359

AIR from ORCHESTRAL SUITE NO. 3 in D-MAJOR*

Bach

Continued on the following page.

Turn to part 360.

* From Edition Eulenburg no. 818. Reprinted by permission of C. F. Peters Corp., sole selling agents in the U.S.A.

Ternary form is even more widely used. An expanded version of the form is the basis of many movements of symphonies, particularly first movements. In this expanded format, a large section of music is presented, new musical material is introduced, and then the original music is brought back again in slightly altered form. Instead of ternary, it is called SONATA-ALLEGRO because of its predominant use in the allegro movements of sonatas and the fact that many other musical devices are employed.

Here is the melody line from part of Haydn's "Symphony No. 94 in G-Major," the third movement. The movement is not in sonata-allegro form, but is ternary. The initial presentation and the return to the "A" section (slightly altered) have been marked.

Turn to part 361.

361

SYMPHONY NO. 94 in G-MAJOR, THIRD MOVEMENT

Haydn

Turn to part 362.

You have now completed chapter 7. Before proceeding to the next chapter, do each of the activities described below, and take the Self-Test. They will help you retain the knowledge just acquired and translate it into useable skills.

Proficiency Developers

1. Turn to "America the Beautiful" (part 251) and identify the four phrases of the song. Then identify their cadences with roman numerals and by name.

2. Try identifying phrases and cadences in the song "When Johnny Comes Marching Home" (part 328), which is in a minor tonality.

3. With your left hand play the I chord in a key of your choice on the piano, followed by the V chord. Then do it again while creating your own melody with the right hand. The melody will probably sound best if you begin and end on some note of the chord being played. Try it several times. Then reverse the cadence (V to I) and do the same thing.

4. Identify the form of at least five songs in another song book.

5. Turn to each song listed in part 343 and identify the properties that give it its form.

6. Turn to the song "The Naughty Boy" in parts 364 and 365. Examine it carefully and determine the form.

Turn to part 363.

7. Look at the following song. Where do the phrases end? What cadences are used at the ends of phrases? How many phrases are there? Are they similar or quite different from each other?

THE SQUIRREL*

Edmund F. Soule

Fast

Whis-ky, fris-ky, hip-pi-ty hop, Up he goes to the tree-top! Whir-ly, twir-ly, round and round. Down he scam-pers to the ground!

Please go to part 364.

*Used with permission, Edmund F. Soule, University of Oregon, Eugene, Oregon.

364

THE NAUGHTY BOY*

John Keats   Edmund F. Soule

Fairly fast

There was a naugh-ty boy, And a naugh-ty boy was he,— He ran a-way to Scot-land the peo-ple for to see. Then he found that the ground was as hard, That a yard was as long,— That a

Continued in part 365.

*Used with permission, Edmund F. Soule, University of Oregon, Eugene, Oregon.

365

song was as mer-ry, That a cher-ry was as red, *rall.*

That lead was as weigh-ty, That four-score was *a tempo*

eigh-ty, That a door was as wood-en As in Eng-land.

So he stood in his

Continued on the following page.

Turn to the next page.

366

« Just for Fun »

The following song is written so that each of the five lines represents a different instrument, but when sung together their harmonies blend. Try singing each line separately. Then, slowly increase the number of lines until five people or five groups are singing all five lines simultaneously.

THE ORCHESTRA SONG

1. The vi - o - lin's play - ing, tra - la - la - la -
2. The clar - i - net, the clar - i - net goes doo-dle, doodle, doodle,
3. The trum - pet is sound - ing ta ta ta ta ta ta ta ta ta
4. The horn, the horn sounds so for -
5. The drum drum plays pum pum, the drum drum plays

Continued on the following page.

Please go to part 367.

Self-Test

On the left are eight musical terms, and on the right are six definitions. Pick the correct definition for each of the terms. (Some definitions will be used more than once.)

1. _____ motive
2. _____ ternary form
3. _____ free form
4. _____ period
5. _____ AB form
6. _____ phrase
7. _____ ABA form
8. _____ binary

A. a form frequently referred to as two-part form, consisting of two main sections of music, both of which may be repeated

B. a brief musical idea or gesture of a few notes length

C. a series of notes that leads to, and reaches a place of resolution or repose such as a cadence

D. a form that follows no set pattern and does not repeat phrases

E. a combination of two phrases

F. a three-part song form involving the idea of establishing a melody, going to a new melody, and then returning to the original

9. What principle is the basis of the ternary form?

Answer the questions in part 368 based on the following song.

① Oh I went down South for to ② see my Sal, Sing ③
Pol-ly Wol-ly Doo-dle all the day, ④ My Sal she am a
⑤ spunk-y gal, Sing Pol-ly Wol-ly Doo-dle all ⑥ the day.

Turn to part 368.

10. _____ What term is used to describe the unit of music between numbers 2 and 3?

11. _____ What term is used to describe the unit of music between numbers 1 and 4?

12. _____ What is the form of this song? (binary, ternary, or free)

13. _____ What term is used to describe the unit of music between numbers 1 and 2?

14. _____ What term is used to describe the unit of music between numbers 4 and 6?

15. _____ Which is longer—a phrase or a period?

16. What is the word we give to the harmonic progressions that help determine phrase endings?

17. Turn to the excerpt from Haydn's "Symphony No. 94" (part 361). Early in the chapter we defined sequences. Locate sequences in two places in the excerpt.

Turn to part 369 for the Answers and Review Index.

Answers & Review Index

1. B (motive defined 336)
2. F (ternary form 343, 351, 353 ff)
3. D (free form 351, 353)
4. E (period 336)
5. A (AB form 351, 353)
6. C (phrase 336)
7. F (ABA form 343, 351, 354 ff)
8. A (binary form 351, 353)
9. The principle of ternary form is "something is stated, there is a departure from it, and then it returns." (ternary form 353, 354)
10. motive (identified 336)
11. phrase (identified 336)
12. binary form (identified 343, 351, 353, 358)
13. motive (identified 336)
14. phrase (identified 336)
15. period (length of 336)
16. cadences (described 349)
17. Sequences are found in the following places:
    —a series of 3; beginning with line 2, measures 4-5
    —a series of 3; beginning with line 5, measure 1, last note
    —a series of 6; beginning with line 5, measure 5
    (sequences identified 336)

8
A Comprehensive View of School Music Programs

370

Competent teachers always begin class with certain goals in mind; let us do the same in this chapter. When you have completed chapter 8, you should be able to do the following:

1. State your present overall goals for teaching music.
2. Name the three musical behaviors and the three learning domains discussed by the author.
3. Identify the seven objectives for a music program, and develop an activity related to each of them.

Musical Behaviors

There are only three activities that are truly musical: (a) listening to music, (b) performing music, and (c) creating music. All other behaviors are less directly involved with music than these three. Of course, we can talk about music, and in some classes teachers talk about it so much that no time is left for anything else. That is an impoverished curriculum. After all, talking about music is talking behavior, not musical behavior. We can also analyze music: dismantle it, examine its rhythms, melodies, dynamics, etc. Analysis contributes to greater musical understanding—we may find more available through our aural senses, or find new and better ways to perform or create music. But as fruitful as analysis may be, it is an analytical behavior, not a musical one.

A good music program centers around the three primary musical behaviors: listening, performing, and creating. Students can listen to good music frequently and intelligently, perform good music alone and with groups, and create music of their own. Music flourishes in our lives because of these behaviors; they are cardinal features of a musical life.

Three Domains of Learning

What aspects of life does education touch? Inevitably, education affects our *knowledge, values,* and *skills*--in music or in any other discipline.

1. *Knowledge* is defined in the dictionary as "the fact or condition of being aware of something." A seemingly limitless number of facts relate to music, so teachers obviously have a great deal of selecting to do. Successful teachers and students have at least one thing in common: they can distinguish between facts of greater and lesser importance. For example, one kind of knowledge involves low-level thought processes, i.e., little more than remembering, naming, memorizing, or identifying something. Of greater importance and value are the high-level thought processes that allow students to use the knowledge, i.e., evaluate, analyze, create, compare, and so on. *It is this utilization to enhance life that makes knowledge valuable.* Students deserve frequent opportunities to develop high-level thought processes, and only rarely should they be left with nothing more than a memorized fact. Here are some words that usually reflect high-level and low-level thought processes.

Words that Indicate High-Level Thought Processes		Words that Indicate Low-Level Thought Processes	
compare	develop	recall	match
analyze	propose	recognize	rephrase
create	plan	identify	quote
modify	originate	remember	describe
predict	calculate	define	list
deduce	verify	memorize	repeat
discover	substantiate	name	locate
interpret	discuss		

2. *Values* are inextricably part of learning. We rarely ever learn without simultaneously forming opinions or making judgments. When we learn something new, we automatically decide whether it is positive or negative in value, and how important or unimportant it is. Of course, these judgments may change as circumstances change, but the point is that we all make such judgments continually and automatically.

As the illustration shows, how we "feel" about what we learn determines our actions. One who learns a great deal about a subject--while acquiring an intense dislike for it--will probably find no use for the distasteful stuff. On the other hand, one who learns even a little about something and finds it very worthwhile will not only use what has been learned, but will seek to expand and enlarge competencies in that area as long as a positive reaction is maintained.

Past experiences and
environmental influences

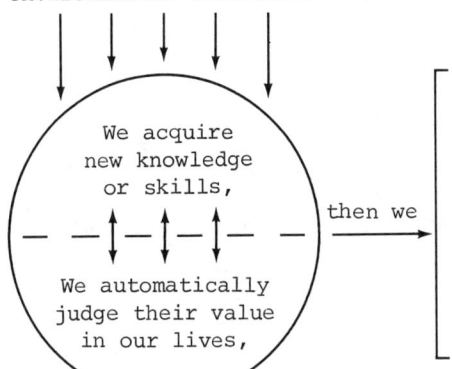

```
    We acquire
   new knowledge
     or skills,
    — -↕-↕-↕- —     then we
   We automatically
   judge their value
      in our lives,
```

- file them to be forgotten quickly, *or*
- file them just in case they might be needed some day, *or*
- file them for quick retrieval because they have real merit, *or*
- change our life now to accommodate them more fully.

Teachers who support the argument that "it is best just to teach the facts and leave judgments of merit completely alone" are supporting a flawed premise because: (a) All the information about the subject cannot be taught. Selecting certain material is, in itself, evidence that importance has been attributed to it; and (b) Learners *cannot* acquire skills or knowledge without simultaneously developing attitudes on the subject. Both are part of the same process, and value judgments are continually being made, whether we want them or not.

3. *Skills* may be defined as a person's abilities to do things competently. They usually infer physical rather than mental activity. Perhaps a more precise term is "psychomotor skill," which indicates a physical ("motor") process initiated by mental ("psycho") action. Two of the three primary musical behaviors discussed earlier (performing and creating) involve such skills. Musical performance is the most highly visible example, and musical creativity also involves skills, evidenced by the creator's performing the sounds, or composing them on paper for others to perform.

To summarize, any comprehensive plan for a school music program will emphasize the three primary musical behaviors: listening, performing, and creating. At the same time, students and teachers together will develop the three domains of learning: knowledge, values, and skills.

Seven Objectives for Elementary Music

At an early stage, music teachers joined the parade honoring behavioral objectives and continue to champion them today. They are valuable to the extent that they help teachers perceive more clearly what they are trying to accomplish and evaluate these efforts afterward. Clear goals and accurate evaluation are hallmarks of good teaching.

At times, however, stating behavioral objectives can be like the magician's broom in the "Sorcerer's Apprentice": The apprentice commanded the broom to fetch water, but once started, he couldn't get the broom to stop, and he was nearly drowned as a result. We have experienced a similar proliferation of educational objectives, until some teachers can't tell the beginning of their program from the end. By examining large numbers of objectives carefully, however, and organizing them into related clusters, seven primary directions emerge. Each one represents a fundamental part of a good music program. They incorporate the three musical behaviors and the three domains of learning described earlier. Here are the seven primary objectives:

What my students will accomplish musically before they leave elementary school

1. They will learn to enjoy many kinds of music, and will continually seek to increase the number of compositions and the kinds of music they enjoy.

2. They will memorize numerous quality songs that represent the American and other heritages and be able to discuss them intelligently.

3. They will be familiar with many instrumental compositions from several heritages and be able to identify and discuss them intelligently.

4. They will learn to use their singing voices confidently, on pitch, and with musical sensitivity. Eventually, they will learn to sing their own part in harmony with others.

5. They will be able to play at least one musical instrument well enough to play or accompany the melodies of several songs.

6. They will be able to use the four elements of music (pitch, rhythm, timbre, dynamics) (a) to analyze a piece of music and explain how each element is employed to make the piece unique; and (b) to organize the elements into many different musical patterns in compositions of their own, and in a wide variety of musical exercises.

7. They will have opportunities to create many different kinds of music, using different sound sources and organizational procedures.

Objective 1
Valuing Music

The first objective concerns attitude and is placed first because of its paramount importance in all learning. (Attitude, you may remember, was identified as one of the essential domains of learning.) Students will explore on their own only music they value. If they discover value in many kinds of music because of a teacher's influence, their lives will be enhanced to that degree. If they learn to diagram sonata-allegro form accurately, yet hate the symphonies that employ the form, their learning was probably to no avail; our attitude toward any subject determines our future involvement with it.

No teacher controls children's attitudes. How then can the formation of positive attitudes be a primary objective? Interestingly, no teacher controls what a child learns either, but we claim to teach knowledge every day. Actually, all a teacher can do is help students acquire knowledge by (a) placing students in an environment conducive to learning, (b) helping them discover the relevance of the activity in their own lives, and (c) involving them with the material in ways that allow them to experience success.

These three steps also lead to formation of positive values. A stimulating environment, relevant objectives and activities, and successful personal experiences with something new are all effective parts of the attitude-forming process. I would add one other item: let the students see the positive feelings *you* have for music. They need to sense that others are excited about aspects of their school lives too.

We live in a world filled with feelings, moods, and emotions. Music touches this world of feeling in unique ways, and evokes a wide variety of feelings in the listener. Indeed, this capacity to awaken feelings is probably the primary reason most societies have always valued music. So good music teachers will systematically explore the different emotional qualities available through music. For example, how many different ways can music evoke feelings of joy? Is the joy the same with each piece of music, or does it change, even though we still use the same imprecise word to describe it? Many persons find that sensitivity to these wide-ranging (and sometimes subtle) differences among the feelings evoked by music is a valued ability that needs constant development.

Objective 2
Knowing Songs

The second objective deals with song repertoire. No specific song list is recommended, for it should change from community to community, perhaps even from person to person. Nonetheless, songs should be memorized; about ourselves, our ancestors, our festivals and holidays, our traditions, and our neighbors far and near. Much of this singing repertoire should relate to our own lives, but not to the exclusion of music from other cultures. For too long we have neglected music from other parts of the world. Ethnic traditions of Europe, Latin America, Asia, and Africa are replete with high-quality, interesting songs, even if they seem remote on first hearing.

Despite frequent claims, music is not a universal language. Some kinds of music seem as distant as the cultures in which they originate. But as we become familiar with foreign music and perceive its function as an art form, we discover a more fundamental common ground with other peoples--our human nature. Learning about their ways gives us insight about ourselves and our place in the human family.

Here are two songs and stories, dictated to the author by Emily Brown, an Inupiat Eskimo from Fairbanks, Alaska. The material has survived through Mrs. Brown's persistant efforts to preserve her people's culture. With no written language of their own, and with the pervading influence of twentieth century America, particularly on Eskimo youth, much of their tradition survives only in the memories of older generations.

376

KOBUK LOVE SONG*

♩ = 126
Gently

Kootuk

Eskimo: Ah ta rook dung, Ah, ——— Ah ta rook dung, Ah, ———
Phonetic: Ah ta ruck doong, Ah, ——— Ah ta ruck doong, Ah, ———
English: May I be your com-pa-ny, As you gen-tly drift a-long.

Ah ku toam, Ah ku toam, Si vu lin ra num, ———
Ah koo doam, Ah koo doam, See voo lin ra noom, ———
May I sit, May I sit, Hap-pi-ly in your Kay-ak,

Na luk deq tsengt nag, ——— Ah, yee yung Aye.
Na luke lick sent nawg, ——— Ah, yee young Aye.
As you pad-dle ex-pert-ly! Ah, yee yung Aye.

Kuk do wah wah, Kuk do wah wah, Nu vik del loo roo. ———
Kook do rah rah, Kook do rah rah, Nah vick teh loo roo. ———
Throw me in-to your Kay-ak, —— Ev-en if it breaks my bones,

na luk deq tsent nag. ——— Ah yee yung aye,
na luke tick sent nawg. ——— Ah yee young aye,
May I be your com-pa-ny. Ah yee yung aye,

Ah, yee yung Aye, Ah, yee yung Aye.
Ah, yee young Aye, Ah, yee young Aye.
Ah, yee yung Aye, Ah, yee yung Aye.

*Used with permission, Emily Ivanoff Brown, Fairbanks, Alaska.

377

KOBUK LOVE SONG
by *Emily Brown*

A Kobuk Indian family moved into the North Country and settled down to making a living at Shungnak. One member of the family was a beautiful girl. On a particular fall day, this lovely young lady was fishing from the river bank when, coming around the bend, she saw for the first time, a kayak. In the kayak was a handsome young Eskimo man. He had never seen an Indian; she had never seen an Eskimo. He turned his kayak to the shore and they spoke together. They had to use sign language, since neither spoke the language of the other.

The girl invited the boy to meet her family and to eat with them. The boy accepted, and spent many happy hours with them. Gradually they began to understand each other. It became known that the handsome Eskimo was hunting caribou. He invited the girl's father to accompany him on the rest of the trip.

After the caribou hunting trip the young man continued his visit. He fell in love with the Indian girl, and she fell in love with him. They asked for permission to marry. The girl's father, realizing his daughter loved this fine young man, granted their wish. Of course, the Eskimo had to return to his village and receive permission from his father also.

He and his bride-to-be walked to the river together and he got into his kayak. As the girl watched her beloved paddle away from her shore, she wanted to cry. But, instead of sending him away with tears, she sang to him. "The Kobuk Love Song" is the girl's song of farewell, wishing her sweetheart a safe and speedy journey. She assures him that she will wait for him and love him forever.

Some time later, the boy returned and they were wed. This was the first marriage of an Eskimo with an Indian. The descendants of this couple named the village Shungnak, a word that is part Eskimo and part Indian. Shungnak is located in northwestern Alaska, within the Arctic Circle and on the Kobuk River.

378

YONGE'S FIRST CATCH*

with enthusiasm
m.m. = ♪ = 138

Mrs. Willook

Eskimo: A - tang - e! A - tang - e! Man-ack tung - a
Phonetic: Ah- tong - ee Ah - tong - ee Man nack toong - a
English: Now look here! Now look here! I caught a fish,

A - tang - e! A - tang - e! Na - tax nam meek
Ah- tong - ee Ah- tong - ee Nah - tah nah mick
Oh look here! Oh look here! It is a floun - der.

A - tang- e! A - tang - e! ti - vi - ti ta - lax nik- suk,
Ah- tong - ee Ah - tong - ee tee-vee tee ta - lak - nik-soak,
Now look here! Now look here! The hook's a - round her, ya ya,

accel. molto

ya ya, ha ya ya! Kix rak! Kix rak!
ya ya, ha ya ya! Key - gu - ruck Key - gu - ruck
ya ya - ya, ya - ya! Kix rah! Kix rak!

*Used with permission, Emily Ivanoff Brown, Fairbanks, Alaska.

YONGE'S FIRST CATCH
by *Emily Brown*

Yonge,[1] a five-year old Eskimo boy went fishing for the first time with his grandfather out on the ice. His grandfather showed him how to make an opening through the ice with his duk.[2] He showed him how to use an Eskimo ice scoop to pick up the ice chips out of an opening.

Now he was ready to sink his hook down into the ocean depths where the fish was. He jiggled his line over and over again. And . . . all of a sudden his line became taut and he could not hold it up. So he called his grandpa to help him pull it up.

"Grandpa! I caught a fish, it is very heavy and I can't lift my hook up!"

Do you know what he caught? A strange looking flat fish called a flounder.

Yonge was disappointed that his first catch wasn't a real fish. So . . . he cried and said, "Let's put it back in the ocean, grandpa!"

"No! No! Yonge. Your mother's favorite fish is this kind. You can carry it home and give it to her. She will cook it for supper."

Yonge wiped his tears and smiled proudly--as his grandpa hung the flounder over his shoulder. Yonge felt quite contented as he walked home with his first catch.

Drum Accompaniment: This piece was usually accompanied by an eskimo drum. The drum part is shown below:

---

[1] pronounced "Yahng-ee"
[2] pronounced "duke"—an Eskimo chisel

Objective 3
Knowing Instrumental Music

No one can identify every piece of music heard, but all of us know some music so well that we feel at home with it—it has be become part of our lives. Such familiarity, and the ability to talk about the music intelligently, comes with repeated study of individual works, instruments and voices used, elements of music and how they interact, the music's historical and cultural setting, and the feelings it evokes. The student's listening repertoire should include compositions by famous composers of the past; music from the jazz, folk, and rock traditions; music of other cultures; and several new kinds of music. Conscientious exploration of selected pieces from all of these repertoires will lead to the familiarity and competency specified in the objective.

Objective 4
Singing

This objective has been most carefully worded. The world is full of adults who were musically "scarred" by teachers who criticized the way they sang. "The teacher asked me to hum along" . . . "I was always the one who played the cymbal" . . . "I was told I just didn't have a singing voice,"—the story is all too familiar.

How can teachers help the ~~non-singer~~ hesitant singer? To begin with, monotones are extremely rare. Children with singing problems are common, but they are not monotones unless the pitch of their voice never varies. The problem is complex and related to the production of correct pitches at correct times; solutions sometimes take many months, or even years. The following observations might be helpful:

1. Because of the complexity of the problem, most solutions derive from repeated individual instruction. The presence of friends distracts (and may embarrass) the student during regular class time.

2. Nearly all students who can't stay on pitch sing below it. Their speaking voices are frequently low pitched, and they have had very little experience sustaining pitches in the upper part of their vocal range.

3. Instead of forcing the student to match the teacher's pitches, the teacher should match the student's. The child can sing a note, any note, and hold it. When he learns to maintain that pitch consistently, he then sings a note that the teacher matches. After both can sing the same pitch consistently, it is time to explore raising and lowering the pitch together, with the teacher following the student.

4. Most children with singing difficulties seem to solve them better with female teachers than with male teachers. The octave difference in the male voice prohibits exact tone-matching and complicates learning for many inexperienced children. These complications may be eliminated if the child sings with a female teacher.

5. Hesitant singers should work on songs that use only three or four pitches. The songs should be sung often, and in the student's limited range (which frequently does not rise much more than a fifth above middle-C).

The fourth musical objective specifies that students use their voices in four ways: confidently, on pitch, musically, and in harmony with others. The word "confidently" indicates the singer's lack of anxiety or fear of reproach. The voice should be clear and normal. "On pitch" indicates accuracy of tone production, i.e., the singer will be able to sing a melody correctly in a given key. The descriptive term "musically" implies that a singer should be able to sing softly or loudly as needed, at the right tempo, and in the right mood. He should not break up musical phrases by breathing indiscriminately or change tone quality abruptly. Other musical improvements may come with maturity but are not essential in these early years. The final part of the objective is "singing in harmony with others." This advanced skill is desirable and widely accomplished by young people, but it may not be achieved early; hence the use of the word "eventually."

In the objective, no reference is made to good tone quality or "beautiful" sounds, nor instructions about body posture, head position, tongue, mouth, or lips. If these are normal, it is enough. If they are obviously abnormal, they need correction. When children meet the standards discussed above, the objective has been met.

Objective 5
Playing Instruments

Experience with musical instruments is important. For some children, simple classroom instruments such as bells, autoharp, ukulele, or recorder will suffice. Others will study the instruments of the orchestra, or perhaps guitar or piano. All such instruments have their place in music, and should be utilized as they become available.

Instruments can be demonstrated in numerous ways. Some instruments, such as the recorder, are basically melody instruments. Others are more suited to playing harmony, such as the autoharp, ukulele, and guitar. Still others have both capabilities: piano, bells, and (for advanced students) guitar. The student may play any instrument to meet this objective, although the broader the playing experience, the better.

Objective 6
Using Musical Elements

By nature, this objective concerns several of the others. If you examine the objectives carefully, nearly all call for student involvement with the elements of music. For example, to value music at more than a primitive level (objective 1), one must perceive the unique and satisfying ways elements are employed to give that music its nature. Discussing, performing, or creating music also demands competency with these elements. Thus, continuous exploration of musical elements throughout the student's musical education is required.

The meaning of each musical element (pitch, rhythm, timbre, dynamics) includes a cluster of important musical characteristics. All characteristics may be explored through the three primary musical behaviors: listening, performing, and creating. Here are a few:

Rhythm

1. basic underlying pulse
2. speech rhythms
3. accents, and the grouping of beats into units of 2 or 3 or combinations of both
4. identifiable rhythmic patterns in any piece of music
5. combining rhythmic patterns to make larger units
6. meters of 2, 3, 4, 5, 6, and higher
7. tempo and its effect in music
8. rhythm's effect in motives, phrases, and periods
9. syncopation

Pitch

1. Melody (horizontal organization of pitches)
   a. direction: ascending, descending, or varied
   b. step-wise (conjunct) or skip-wise (disjunct) movement
   c. the various scales available for making music
   d. phrases, and their progression toward or from do
   e. register: high or low
   f. levels of tunefulness
   g. diatonic or chromatic patterns of notes
2. Harmony (vertical organization of pitches)
   a. consonance and dissonance, their relative nature
   b. major, minor, atonal, and other organizational schemes
   c. cadences

      d. embellishing melodies (adding harmony to beautify, and reinforce melodic statements)
      e. chord progressions
      f. modulation (moving from one tonality to another)
      g. chords, their names or numbers and functions
3. Texture
      a. monophonic (a single melodic line)
      b. polyphonic (multiple melodies such as rounds, canons, and fugues)
      c. homophonic (melody with less prominent accompaniment)
      d. antiphonal (alternating parts, echo songs)

Timbre or Tone Color

1. characteristic sound of individual instruments and voices
2. standard groups of instruments: strings, woodwinds, brass, percussion
3. combinations of instruments: duet, trio, quartet, quintet, sextet, septet, octet, nonet, and larger groups
      a. groups in which each player has his or her own part: *chamber* groups
      b. in orchestras and other larger groups several players play each part
4. how each sound is produced: what vibrates?

Dynamics

1. many levels of loudness between fortissimo and pianissimo
2. concept of crescendo and decrescendo

The other objectives may be approached one at a time (for example, a teacher may set out to memorize a song with the class or create an original piece of music, and then go on to demonstrate a new instrument) but because all music is made up of elements, this objective becomes omnipresent, even when the primary focus is on another objective. The song being learned will have greater meaning if some attention is given to its rhythms, harmony, tempo, dynamic level, and so on.

Objective 7
Creating Music

Some teachers consider this objective so important that they virtually build their entire music programs around it. When pursued with enough intensity and thoroughness, most of the other objectives will at least be partially explored in the process of learning to create music. What are some of the ways students can create music?

Rhythmic Compositions: These activities use body sounds or rhythm instruments of many kinds. Students may explore meters of 2, 3, 4, 5, or more. Different combinations of 2 and 3 make interesting patterns. Rhythmic pieces can be done as rounds, then in binary or ternary form; in two, three, or four parts. There are dozens of instruments to use, including homemade drums, rattles, and rhythm sticks.

Different Scales: By limiting the student to the notes of any existing scales (or by devising scales of your own), fresh, new sounds can be born. It is easiest to use tone bells with removable bars, or tunable stringed instruments for new scales, rather than trying to play them on fixed-pitch instruments such as the piano or recorder.

Varying Sound Sources: The only limit to sounds used in music today is the creator's imagination. Traditional instruments, homemade instruments, electronic sounds, instruments from other cultures, household objects, objects in nature, and the human voice in numerous manifestations can all be used with rewarding and musical results.

Traditional Songs and Instrumental Pieces: Much successful music can be written in standard formats; setting a nursery rhyme or poem to music, or writing an instrumental piece for standard instruments. Following are two examples of compositions by students preparing to be elementary school teachers; both have creative freshness and musicality.

385

THE ELF IN MYSELF*

Helen Lowrie Marshall
Connie L. McRae

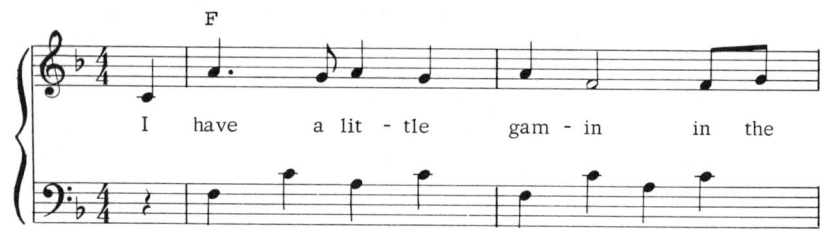

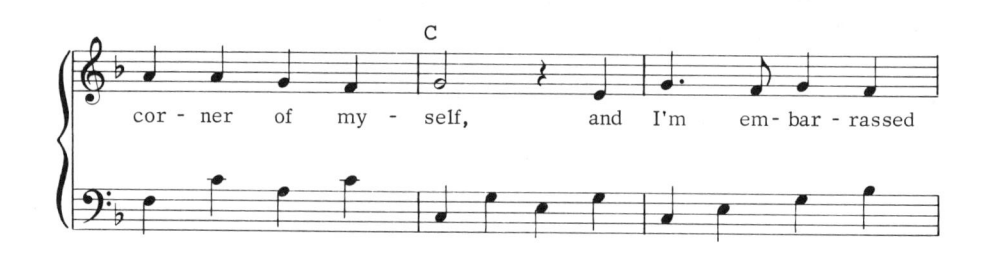

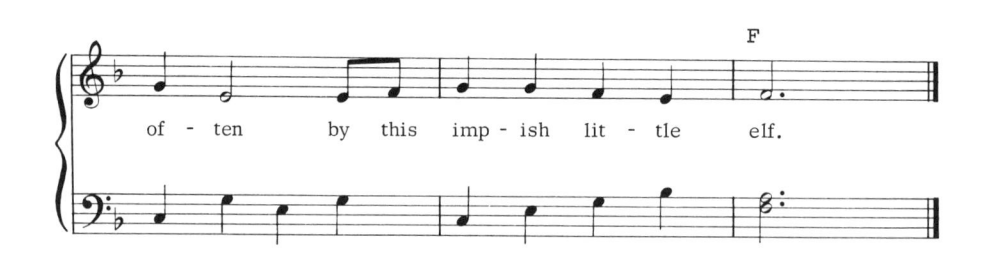

I have a lit-tle gam-in in the cor-ner of my-self, and I'm em-bar-rassed of-ten by this imp-ish lit-tle elf.

2. She's fond of shocking people who are proper as can be.
   Believe me it's not funny. She's a terrible trial to me.

3. But I hope my friends will try to take notice and see.
   It's the gamin who is naughty, and it isn't really me!

*From *Hold to Your Dream*, Helen Lowrie Marshall. Copyright 1965 by Helen Lowrie Marshall. Used by permission of Doubleday and Company, Inc.

386

OLD CHAIRS TO MEND

Sue Foote

If I'd as much mon-ey as I could spend, I never would cry old chairs to mend. Old chairs to mend, old chairs to mend, I never would cry old chairs to mend.

*Used with permission, Sue Foote, Salem, Oregon.

Devised Notation: Many of the sounds in contemporary music defy standard notation, so composers devise notation as they need it. Sometimes the musical staff is still present, but with dots, squiggles, lines of all shapes, blocks, and other patterns designating what is to be played. Other times the notational format resembles a graph or chart more than a musical score. The notation may be very precise in controlling pitches and rhythms, or it may give only general indications, leaving many decisions up to the performer. By providing opportunities for students to devise their own notation for sounds they create, many new approaches to musical composition become possible.

Organizational Procedures: Standard procedures such as binary and ternary forms, theme and variations (A, A^2, A^3, A^4, with each presentation modified in some different way), or rondo form (ABACA or ABACABA) are still very widely used. Other organizational procedures may also be developed, or in some cases the teacher may use no procedure, letting chance be the determiner of events as much as possible.

Summary: The full scope of a good music program can be seen through the many different possible interactions between all of the items that are part of the foregoing discussion. They are listed in abbreviated form below.

Seven Musical Objectives	Three Musical Behaviors	Three Domains of Learning
1. valuing music	1. performing	1. knowledge
2. knowing songs	2. creating	2. values
3. knowing instrumental music	3. listening	3. skills
4. singing		
5. playing instruments		
6. using musical elements		
7. creating music		

« Just for Fun »

Before you go to the Proficiency Developers, try to solve the following puzzle.

MUSICAL ALPHABET SOUP*

Hidden among all these letters are the names of forty *musical instruments*. You can look up, down, left, or right, but they are all hidden there! Circle the words as you find them, and happy hunting.

```
A V E L G U I T A R A G K S
S I D P S M H U U U L G C P
N O R G A N A B K E N L O I
K L B R X D R A U S O A L N
V I O L O N C E L L O S B E
I N B T P T S R E L S S D T
O S O E H R M Y L E S H O M
L I E N O U K L E B A A O A
Y N Z A N M A U N S B R W N
F L U T E P Z O O N E M C D
L C O S V E O J N A B O Y O
A L Q A U T O H A R P N M L
U A X C H E L U T E R I B I
T R O M B O N E J D E C A N
P I A N O O T L A R C A L T
I N E N O H P A S U O S S E
C E L E O B O R E M R A S N
C T I S I T A R R A D I O O
O I T E N R O C N O E B T R
L O I V S S A B A R R I L T
O N A R P O S E P I P G A B
```

(See part 413 for the answers.)

*Used with permission, Karen Kammerer, University of Oregon, Eugene, Oregon.

Proficiency Developers

1. Objective 6, Using Musical Elements, discussed four musical elements and several characteristics for each. Divide a sheet into four parts, one for each element. Then list as many musical characteristics as you can for each element. Compare your list to the one in part 382-383.

2. In the discussion of musical knowledge (domains of learning) two levels of thought processes were identified, high and low. List as many words as you can that promote high-level and low-level thought processes. Compare your list to the one in part 371. Did you use words other than those on the list? That's all right, many others do exist.

3. Two domains of learning are knowledge and values. Describe in two or three sentences the relationship between the two. How often is one acquired without the other? Compare your answer to the discussion beginning in part 371, number 2.

4. One of the real challenges of a music teacher is the young, hesitant singer. List as many ways as you can to help such a child overcome this problem. Discuss your list with someone who has had experience working with such students. And reread the author's suggestions beginning in part 380.

5. Look at the songs "Long, Long Ago" (part 390) and "Sleep Baby Sleep" (part 392). What can you say about the various musical elements in each song? Is the meter constant? Are certain rhythmic patterns used more than once? Is the song in a major key? Is its tempo appropriate for the lyrics? What other statements can you make about each song?

Please go to part 393.

390

LONG, LONG AGO*

Slow　　　　　　　　　　　　　　　　　　　　　Edmund F. Soule

1. Winds thru the ol-ive trees soft-ly did blow, Round lit-tle Beth-le-hem Long, long a-go.
2. Sheep on the hill-side lay whit-er than snow, Shep-herds were watch-ing them long, long a-go.
3. Then from the hap-py sky, an-gels bent low,
4. For in a man-ger bed, Cra-dled we know,

*Used with permission, Edmund F. Soule, University of Oregon, Eugene, Oregon.

391

sing - ing their songs of joy— long,—
Christ— came to Beth - le - hem,— Long,

long,— long— a - go.—
long,— long— a go.—

392

SLEEP, BABY, SLEEP*

fairly slow　　　　　　　　　　　　　　　Edmund F. Soule

Sleep, ba-by, sleep! Thy fa-ther watch-es the sheep. Thy moth-er is shak-ing the dream-land tree, And down falls a lit-tle dream on thee. O sleep baby, sleep, baby sleep.

*Used with permission, Edmund F. Soule, University of Oregon, Eugene, Oregon.

Self Evaluation Test

Although many activities relate to music in some way, three musical behaviors are primary. What are the three primary musical behaviors?

1.
2.
3.

When students begin learning about any subject, teachers must include three areas or domains of learning in their curriculum. What are the three domains?

4.
5.
6.

Chapter 8 identified seven objectives of a good elementary music program. State those seven objectives.

7.
8.
9.
10.
11.
12.
13.

One of the objectives relates to the elements of music. What are these four elements of music?

14.
15.
16.
17.

Turn the page to part 394.

Answers & Review Index

1. listening (primary musical behaviors 370)
2. performing (370)
3. creating (370)
4. knowledge (three domains of learning 371)
5. values (371)
6. skills (371)
7. They will learn to enjoy many kinds of music (musical objectives 374)
8. They will memorize a large number of quality songs (375)
9. They will be able to identify a large number of musical compositions by name (380)
10. They will use their singing voices confidently (380)
11. They will play one or more musical instruments (381)
12. They will use the elements of music in several ways (382)
13. They will create several different kinds of music (383)
14. pitch (elements of music 382)
15. rhythm (382)
16. timbre (383)
17. dynamics (383)

9
Becoming the Right Kind of Teacher

This chapter will discuss (a) the nature of learning behavior; (b) motivation; (c) teacher and student roles in learning activities; (d) two teaching strategies and rationale to indicate which strategy provides the greater advantage for students; and (e) several different learning activities—not ready-made lessons for the teaching day, but illustrations of activities teacher and students can devise together.

When the chapter is completed you should be able to do the following:

1. Describe a good learning environment and student and teacher roles in that environment.
2. Describe two primary teaching strategies in use today, including the five steps of the student-oriented strategy.
3. Apply the RULEG system to music objectives.
4. Write a behavioral objective for music that states (a) what the student will do, (b) how well it must be done, and (c) the circumstances under which it will be performed.

Nature of Learning

According to one prominent psychological theory, learning occurs only when one perceives a gap between the present condition and where one wants to be, and so makes adjustments to close that gap. If something as significant as wanting to become a teacher, lawyer, or engineer is involved, closing the gap involves many years of diligent work. More frequently, however, less consequential goals are at stake, such as wanting to determine the shortest or fastest route home or the proper way to operate some kind of equipment. It is also possible to learn things not for their own value, but to satisfy a secondary desire: combing your hair to please a member of the opposite sex rather than yourself, or studying hard because you desire a high grade rather than desiring knowledge. In any case, the theory, illustrated below, seems to have validity.

CONDITION THAT
INITIATES LEARNING

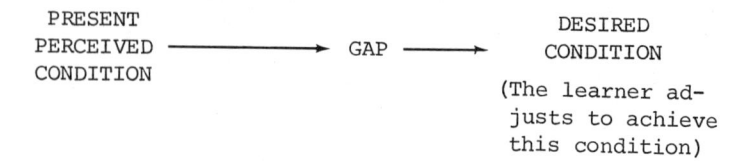

PRESENT
PERCEIVED ⟶ GAP ⟶ DESIRED
CONDITION   CONDITION
                    (The learner ad-
                    justs to achieve
                    this condition)

Motivation

Two central ideas emerge in the theory just illustrated: (a) we learn when we perceive a *gap* or *imbalance* in our lives, and (b) we learn by *doing*, i.e., the learner is the one who adjusts, or learns—no one else can do it for him. The theory, therefore, seems to have its roots in motivation, the one factor that pervades all learning. Motivation might be defined as the desire or need to restore balance, or close a perceived gap. Good teaching always instills motivation in learners. Success depends on it; failure is marked by its absence.

Learners can be motivated by activity itself—called *intrinsic motivation* because it is part of the activity. The person who studies the music of Mozart because she enjoys it is said to have intrinsic motivation. The person who is not interested in the music of Mozart, but studies it anyway because of grades, parental pressure, diplomas, or any other reason not part of the original activity, is said to have *extrinsic motivation*. Both types are effective and useful to some degree, but the former is more fundamental and direct.

What is the learner's role in this process? Above all, the learner must be active, a doer, a participant--one who feels the need to close the perceived gap, execute the learning activity, and frequently plan it. The learner acquires new knowledge, skills, or attitudes.

The teacher's role is different. The teacher is an organizer, motivator, and resource. She facilitates the learners' activities while they learn. Good teaching is not so much dispensing information as it is determining students' activities, understanding the nature of their learning tasks, organizing and arranging the learning environment, and facilitating their efforts to learn.

All teachers share at least one common tendency: We feel responsible to fill class time. We feel obligated to take charge, to "give the students" what they need. And when we don't do these things, guilt feelings arise for shirking our responsibility. These tendencies get teachers in trouble as often as they help them, for they sometimes result in authoritarian presentation-modes not conducive to learning, and on occasion actually prevent learning in all but the most persistent students. The issue becomes clearer when we list a teacher's goals to facilitate learning:

1. The teacher can define the task so that the learner knows precisely what is needed to acquire competency.
2. The teacher can demonstrate the value of the competency in her life, and the lives of others.
3. The teacher can place the learner in a situation that aids acquisition of the competency.
4. The teacher can show the consequences of living without the competency.

After the teacher accomplishes these goals, *the learner must acquire the competency himself*. The teacher does not have control of that final, essential step. If the student does not take the final step, the teacher's previous efforts have little meaning. The process applies to values and skills as well as knowledge. Learning should always be learner-oriented, not teacher-oriented.

Teaching Strategies for Music

The teaching strategies employed in other disciplines are also pertinent to music classes. Two common strategies are called the teacher-oriented *presentational mode*, and the student-oriented *activity mode*. (Some music specialists also need to develop strategies for conducting music rehearsals, but such rehearsal techniques are not within the scope of this book.)

For many centuries the presentational (or lecture) mode dominated education, and was in turn dominated by the teacher preparing and presenting the lectures. Today, it is still stubbornly entrenched in education despite evidence indicating its lack of success, at least in terms of students' abilities to apply knowledge to new situations and to solve problems.

To prepare and present a thirty-minute lecture on some aspect of music, the teacher must determine goals, analyze the music, discover the relationships among the musical elements, gather together good examples, organize the material, and finally present everything to the class. Each step is a good learning activity for the teacher. The teacher's perceived gap is the class time that must be filled and the motivation derives from her desire to excel at the task. When the teacher fills the class time, the gap is bridged—for the teacher. At best, the student was paying attention and taking notes. At worst, the student was mentally miles away, on a beach or with a friend. Most often, the teacher is the primary beneficiary of this classroom situation, and feelings of accomplishment lead her to the erroneous judgment that the presentation was a good learning experience for everyone in the room, whether or not the students were involved. Interestingly, students who look back on their outstanding lecturers frequently remember the excitement and respect engendered by the teacher's performances more clearly than they remember the content of the lectures.

Not that teachers should avoid the presentational mode altogether. People communicate with words. We learn by talking to each other. At times the best way to learn something is to have someone tell you what you need to know. The key word here is "need." The student must feel the need before he will hear what is said to him, and have the opportunity to try the behavior unassisted before he can call it his own. So a good class could have several short presentations by the teacher during any given hour when the need arises, each presentation aimed at creating new possibilities for the students in their learning activity.

Two fallacies encourage teachers to use the presentational mode predominantly:

1. More material can be covered if ideas are organized and spoken without interruption in front of the class.

2. Students "learn" what the teacher knows, if she says what she knows before a group of them.

Fallacy 1: Education is not concerned with the amount of material that is *presented* in classrooms, but rather with the amount of material students possess as individuals, and even more important, how they can *use* the material in life. Lectures that seem highly efficient to the teacher because so much is "covered" (spoken?) in the classroom may in reality be dishearteningly inefficient because of the small amount students actually assimilate and use over the long term.

Fallacy 2: Research indicates that people remember very poorly what is said in front of them. In fact, the lecture is one of the teacher's weaker tools. We cannot assume someone has effectively learned anything until that person demonstrates in some way the ability to use it. Teachers' gullibility is a continuing source of amazement when they assume something has been "learned" by their students because it was "taught" in a recent lecture.

The student-oriented activity mode avoids many of these pitfalls. In good student-oriented classes, several factors promote learning. The following cycle demonstrates these positive factors.

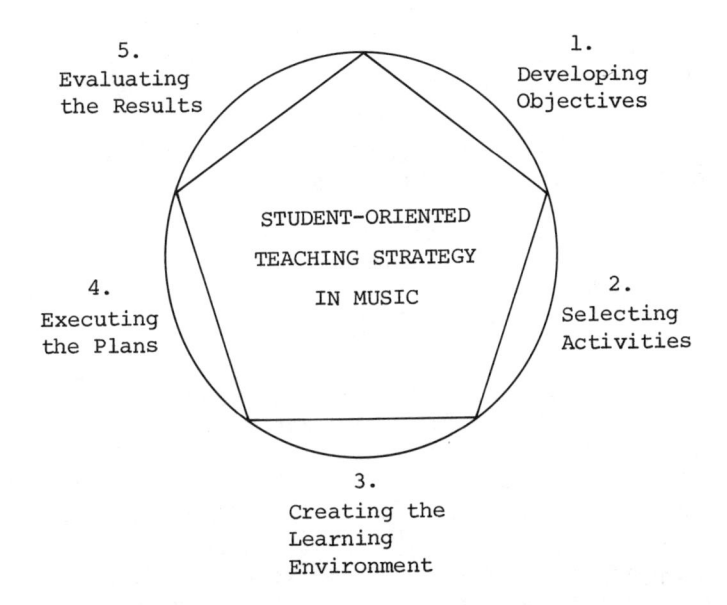

```
         5.                              1.
    Evaluating                      Developing
    the Results                     Objectives


                 STUDENT-ORIENTED
                 TEACHING STRATEGY
      4.            IN MUSIC             2.
    Executing                        Selecting
    the Plans                        Activities


                       3.
                  Creating the
                    Learning
                  Environment
```

Developing Objectives

With the student-oriented strategy, goal-setting is a process of interaction between teacher *and* students. In other words, the students are directly involved in determining the subject matter. Because goals are stated as student behaviors, the orientation of the whole learning process is on the students' performances.

Behavioral Objectives: Teachers are steadily realizing that goal-ambiguity is one of the most common weaknesses in the learning process. The ambiguity is partially caused by teachers who do not set specific goals at all or set objectives that lack clarity. Ideally, an objective will be clear on the following points:

1. It will specify the *kind of behavior* accepted as evidence that the learner achieved the objective. (What will the student *do* to show that the material was learned?)
2. It will specify the *conditions* under which the behavior will occur. (When and where will the student demonstrate the competency?)

3. It will describe *how well* the learner must do the task. (What specific standards of performance must the student achieve?)

Example: As part of the final examination, the student will play the harmony for "This Land Is Your Land" on the autoharp, using the correct chords, and at an appropriate tempo for singing.

1. The behavior described is "playing the harmony."
2. The conditions are that the student will play a specified song, and that it will be played on the autoharp during the final examination.
3. How well the student is to play is specified as "using correct chords, and at an appropriate tempo for singing."

All objectives can be substantially improved by specifying the student's behavior; the conditions and standard of performance may not be as vital to classroom success in some situations. All three should, of course, be employed whenever they are useful.

The words we use to describe behavior are very important. Some words are so vague and all-inclusive, they have very little meaning. The following example illustrates the point.

Words Open to Many Interpretations	Words With More Specific Meanings
to know	to write
to understand	to recite
to really understand	to analyze
to appreciate	to differentiate between
to grasp the significance	to describe
to enjoy	to construct
to believe	to perform
to master	to solve
to comprehend	to match

An objective that avoids the vague words in the left column and meets the three criteria described above is a behavioral objective. It will help teachers determine whether their students are actually learning what they are supposed to be learning.

Scope of Objectives: How much time and energy should be spent on each objective? How deep should the class probe? How wide-ranging should the search be? For example, if the objective is to identify musical instruments, will the class listen only to symphony orchestra instruments, or will other instruments be added from the traditions of rock and jazz, electronics, or other cultures? The answer depends on several factors: the time available, the relative importance of each objective, its relationship to the entire music program and the resources available. All of these factors may serve as criteria for decisions about the use of time, money, and energy in the music program.

Sequence of Objectives: Because the school term stretches over many months, teachers and students are confronted with numerous goals that must be approached in some sequence. There are widely varying opinions on how the sequence of learning activities should be determined. Some frequently suggested organizational formats are as follows:

1. Simple to Complex. Especially with younger or less experienced students, simple ideas basic to the topic must precede more complex ideas. After the simpler concepts are acquired, ideas that entail greater precision or a more encompassing view of the topic can be introduced.

2. Known to Unknown. Students perform better in learning situations that begin where they have experienced some success or accomplishment. Once that frame of reference is established, it is easier to move into related, unexplored areas of activity.

3. Whole to Part. Often, learners can deal with material as a whole, later dividing it into parts, each to be examined in increasing detail. For example, it is possible to discuss a musical composition generally, later examine several individual elements, and finally explore any one aspect in great detail.

Whichever sequence is used, students should perceive some *continuity* between their objectives and recognize how the many facets of learning *integrate* into a chosen professional skill or life style.

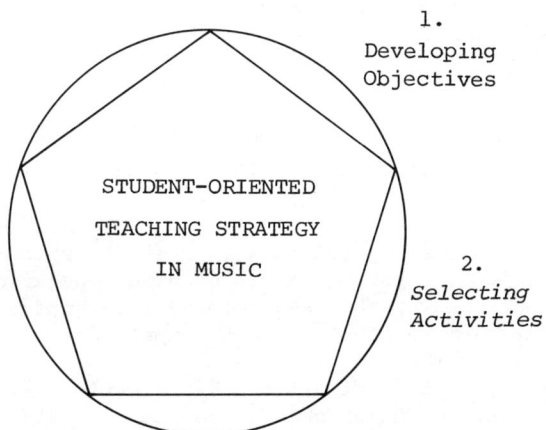

1. Developing Objectives

STUDENT-ORIENTED TEACHING STRATEGY IN MUSIC

2. *Selecting Activities*

Selecting Activities

Teachers should exercise sound judgment in selecting activities to help students meet their established goals. A series of questions need to be asked about any proposed activity. First, "Is the activity desirable or important to the learners?" If so, the motivation for action is inherent in its completion. On the other hand, there is very little hope of students achieving goals if their class activities possess no such intrinsic motivation. Second, "If the students complete the activity, will they possess the competencies specified in the objective?" Many times, completion of a classroom activity only approximates the specified behavior. Third, "Is the activity within the student's capability?" If not, an intermediate objective is probably necessary. For example, assume a teacher has the following objective: *The students will be able to create their own four-note ostinatos appropriate for the song* "A Frog Went A-Courting." If the activity selected to meet the objective has everyone working together to create the ostinato, many students may still lack the ability to complete the objective alone. The ostinato is a cooperative effort between teacher and students, and the presence of the ostinato does not mean the objective is met by each individual. Thus, some intermediate objectives might be appropriate, like the following:

1. Each student will devise a four-note ostinato based on the notes, D, E, F♯, and A.

2. Each student will play his ostinato on some instrument for the class.

3. Each student will select four notes that might be used as part of an ostinato for the song "A Frog Went A-Courting," and explain why those notes are appropriate.

4. Each student will find at least two places in the song where the notes of the ostinato might change.

These intermediate objectives will help students reach the original objective through a process the teacher can share. Learning will be visible, success achieved frequently, and the teacher will know much more about student competencies.

To summarize, if the activity (a) is accepted by the students as worthwhile, (b) demands a demonstration of the ability described in the objective, and (c) is within the capability of the students, it is the right activity.

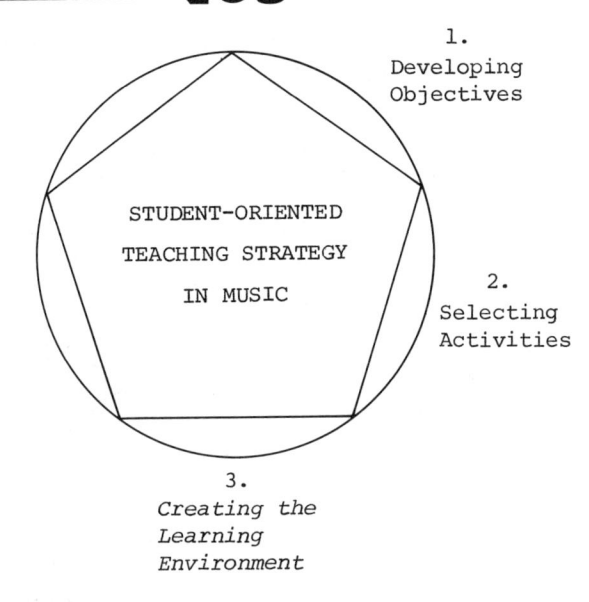

```
                    1.
                  Developing
                  Objectives


     STUDENT-ORIENTED
     TEACHING STRATEGY      2.
         IN MUSIC         Selecting
                          Activities



              3.
           Creating the
           Learning
           Environment
```

Creating the Proper Learning Environment

Both the physical and psychological environments need the teacher's attention. Beside the proper heating, lighting, ventilation, and visibility in the room, the sound equipment used in class is very important. Music as an art form thrives or withers on the basis of quality. Poor-quality records or faulty phonograph equipment or tape recorders can, by themselves, ruin an otherwise excellent lesson. High-quality sound equipment is so important, it should be checked out before every class.

Printed materials are also important. Although the quality of elementary music materials is continually improving, some books and song collections are better than others. The teacher should investigate these materials carefully, making selections based on local needs. If more than one series of books is available, the curriculum will obviously be enhanced.

The psychological environment is probably more important to learning than the physical. Good learning environments are made by the teacher's approach to learning. It is very important that students perceive (a) a constant desire for an *open* exchange of ideas, opinions, and questions in the classroom, and (b) an atmosphere completely *free from fear* of revealed ignorance or mistakes. Only when we are free to make mistakes and overcome our revealed inadequacies without threat can we devote full attention to the accomplishment of our goals. If students perceive that their mistakes and inadequacies will be ridiculed or punished, their energies will be primarily devoted to defending against such exposure, either by pretending understanding or defying the teacher. Mistakes are a normal part of learning and not to be dwelt on; they provide new directions for the learner. Finally, when correct performance occurs in class, (c) *positive reinforcement* in some form is also important. Most often it will take the form of just a brief acknowledgment such as "good," "that's right," or "O.K.," but frequent positive reinforcement has long range benefits if it is genuine and unobtrusive.

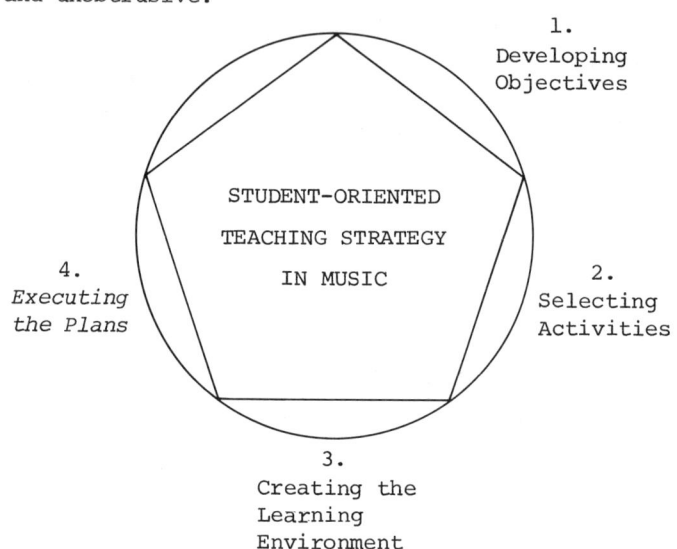

```
                           1.
                      Developing
                      Objectives

           STUDENT-ORIENTED
           TEACHING STRATEGY
   4.         IN MUSIC            2.
Executing                      Selecting
the Plans                      Activities

              3.
         Creating the
           Learning
         Environment
```

Students Execute the Planned Activity

The teacher's role in this fourth step is a colearner, resource person, or coordinator of activities while the students are busy acquiring skills, knowledge, and concomitant attitudes. If the cycle's first three steps have been properly accomplished, this step is simply the culmination of these earlier activities. The teacher may find occasional presentation and demonstration desirable, but during activities the teacher should be "on the sidelines" as much as possible. In this stage true student-orientation or teacher-orientation is determined.

No two planned educational activities are exactly alike. Nevertheless, most are confined to the 45-50 minute class period or less. The school bell can exercise true tyranny over learning if teachers allow it. The solution is not difficult for the persistent teacher—he must be certain the students (and their objectives) determine how long the class remains with an activity, not an arbitrary time schedule. If the activity spills over into the class time of the next day, the teacher should let it do so and readjust the class's future plans. Much important learning is never achieved because time runs out, and the next day's schedule calls for the class to go on to another activity.

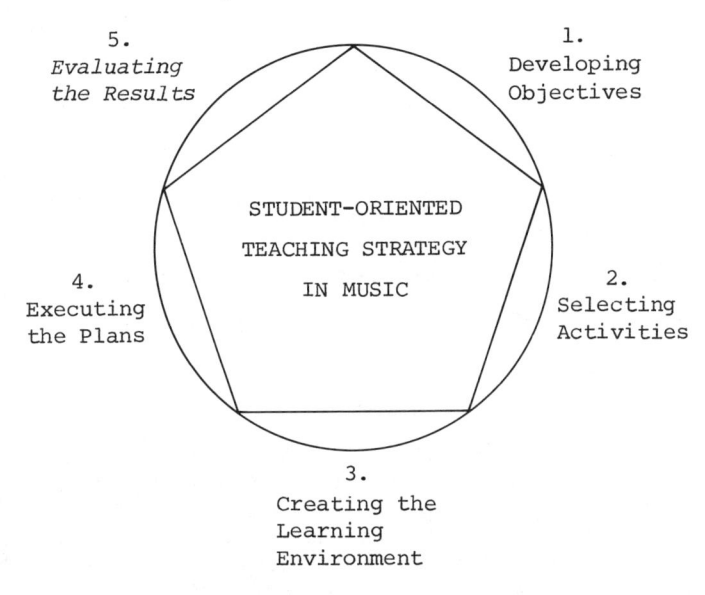

```
        5.                                    1.
     Evaluating                           Developing
     the Results                          Objectives


                    STUDENT-ORIENTED
                    TEACHING STRATEGY
        4.             IN MUSIC              2.
     Executing                            Selecting
     the Plans                            Activities


                         3.
                    Creating the
                    Learning
                    Environment
```

Evaluation of the Entire Process

Evaluation includes not only the measurement of student success, but also the appropriateness of the original objectives, the quality of the activities selected, the created physical and psychological environment, and the students' execution of the plans. Any of these steps may—indeed, probably will—be changed in some way for subsequent classes as the result of a thorough evaluation.

It is important to evaluate the learning process at this stage of the cycle because of the availability of information about the whole process, but the teacher should also make evaluations throughout all stages. The evaluations may even extend beyond school activities. Here, for example, is a list of criteria used by one teacher to evaluate singing in an elementary music program.

How to Evaluate Classroom Singing

1. Have the children memorized a variety of songs useable in different kinds of social and school activities?

2. Do the children want to sing at home?
3. Do they enjoy singing at school and participate willingly?
4. Have you taken steps to help the hesitant singers?
5. Do the students have opportunities to sing songs they like?
6. Do they have opportunities to use creative imagination in the way songs are performed and accompanied?
7. Can they sing one part of the music while other students sing other parts?
8. Can they talk intelligently about the music they sing, its elements, and history?
9. Do they have opportunities to be the musical leader?
10. Is the pitch of their voices usually accurate?

Preparation by the teacher is one sure sign of good instruction. Entering class without clearly organized plans of activity leaves success purely to chance. Here is a sample lesson plan format. Compare it to the teaching strategy cycle in part 405. Although the wording varies, it follows the same basic format and is based on the same principles. One last note: Such plans are positive influences unless they become inflexible and impervious to unanticipated student questions and interests. Unanticipated teaching moments need our attention and flexible response, even if it means departing briefly from previously formed plans.

Lesson Plan Outline

Class: Date:

Objectives (behaviorally stated):

Materials and Equipment:

Procedure (explanations, activities, etc.)

Evaluation (of the activity)
           (of the students)

The RULEG System of Selecting Classroom Experiences

RULEG is an acronym that combines the RUL from "rule," and the Latin designation for the word "for example," E.G. It refers to the process of stating a rule, and then giving several examples of that rule in operation. For the music teacher, it means stating an objective or principle for students to master, and then describing several activities (examples) that will develop that mastery. An illustration follows:

> RULE: It is important for students to identify meters of two and three when heard, and to create their own rhythmic patterns in each meter. (Note that this statement contains *two* behaviors: identifying and creating.)

Identifying

Example 1: The teacher will play short excerpts from six musical selections. After each selection a student will identify it as duple or triple, and the class will discuss briefly why it is so grouped.

Example 2: The teacher will clap several rhythmic patterns in two or three, and students will identify them as duple or triple. Different students will explain why the meter is so grouped.

Example 3: Individual students will recite nursery rhymes before the class for all to determine their meter. Others will identify the meter and explain why it is so grouped. For example, "Jack and Jill" = duple, "Jack Sprat" = duple, "Hey Diddle Diddle" (recited slowly) = triple, "Little Miss Muffet" (recited slowly) = triple.

Example 4: The teacher will clap duple and triple patterns (changing frequently from one to the other without a pause between) while at the same time class members hold up two fingers or three fingers to signify the meter.

Creating

Example 1: Class members will agree on a song in duple or triple meter (either recorded or played by the teacher). They will then select rhythmic instruments and create an accompaniment to the song. When the accompaniment is completed, another group of students with different instruments will create a new accompaniment for the same song. After several such exercises the variety of rhythmic possibilities will be discussed by the students.

Example 2: The class will create a rhythmic composition of sixteen measures, using body sounds (claps, stamps, snaps, and so on) in duple or triple meter. They will rehearse it as a group several times. Then the teacher will make a round out of it by starting part of the class at the beginning, and starting other groups four, eight, and twelve measures later.

Example 3: The class will create a rhythmic composition in ternary form.

1. Determine a meter
2. Divide the class into two groups, and have members of each group select instruments. Use different instruments in the two groups as much as possible.
3. Have group A create a composition of about 16 measures length for their instruments. Do the same for group B.
4. Experiment with various tempos and dynamic levels to determine the rhythm and loudness of various parts of the music.
5. Have group A play, followed by group B without any break between the two groups. When group B finishes, group A repeats its part again. The resulting composition is in ABA (ternary) form, and in the selected meter.

The teacher now has seven activities for students, all of which help develop the competencies described in the RULE. Each activity relates closely to the objective, and gives the students experience in approaching musical principles from many different directions.

The RULEG system is applicable to any aspect of music. It first states important principles, and then systematically develops activities to achieve their mastery. The variety of activities developed over a period of time brings flexibility to the teaching-learning process, and increases substantially the chances of successful musical learning in the classroom.

« Just for Fun »

Before you begin the Proficiency Developers, try your hand with some Picturewords.

PICTUREWORDS*

Words can often be made to look like the thing they describe. Here are some examples of what I mean:

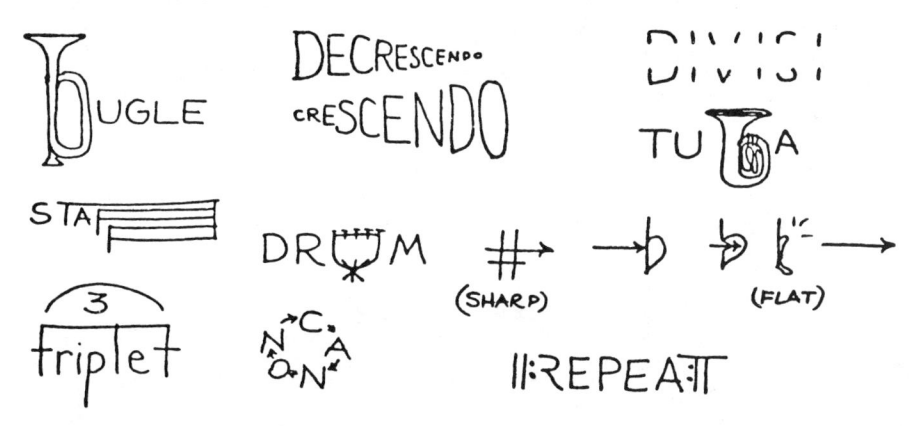

[bugle, decrescendo, crescendo, divisi, tuba, staff, drum, sharp, flat, triplet, D.C. al fine (con), repeat]

... you get the idea. Now see what *you* can do with the musical words listed below:

scale	staccato	solo
chord	piano	duet
note	fortissimo	baton
fugue	rest	da capo
saxophone	fermata	gong
ostinato	presto	accent
pentatonic	symphony	bow
tie	horn	tutti
slur	dolce	sforzando
tremolo	trill	ritard
vibrato	vivace	accellerando
largo	trombone	key

(Look these up in a music dictionary! Often the definitions will give you some ideas about ways they can be made into Picturewords.)

*Used with permission, Karen Kammerer, Oregon, Eugene, Oregon.

Proficiency Developers

1. Review the three components of a behavioral objective as described in part 399. Then write a behavioral objective for each of the four elements of music, or for a subcategory of each of the seven objectives of musical programs (chapter 8).

2. When working with behavioral objectives, the teacher must learn to avoid vague and ambiguous descriptors. Form a list of vague descriptors in one column (e.g., "know"), and precise ones in another column (e.g., "write"). Compare your list to the one in part 400.

3. Review the list of criteria for singing found in parts 405-406. Then pick out one element from part 382, and develop a similar list of criteria to evaluate your teaching of it.

4. Select one subheading for each element from those shown in part 382. Using the RULEG system, state it as a rule, and develop four or five activities to achieve its mastery.

Self-Test

According to the psychological theory described in the book, learning occurs only when a certain circumstance exists. What is that circumstance?

   1.

Name the two teaching strategies discussed in this chapter.

   2.
   3.

Three components are necessary in behavioral objectives. Describe each of them briefly.

   4.
   5.
   6.

Student-oriented teaching strategy is comprised of five cyclical steps. In order, describe each in two or three words.

   7.
   8.
   9.
 10.
 11.

411

When a teacher selects activities for the class, the activities should meet three criteria. Identify each criterion with one sentence or less.

12.
13.
14.

Identify three factors that promote a positive psychological environment in the classroom.

15.
16.
17.

One of the teacher's tasks is to put the class's objectives in some rational, workable sequence. What three methods of establishing a sequence were suggested in this chapter?

18.
19.
20.

Please turn to part 412 for Answers and Review Index.

Answers & Review Index

1. People learn when they perceive a gap between their present circumstance and their desired circumstance. (motivation 395-396)
2. Student-oriented teaching strategy (397-399)
3. Teacher-oriented teaching strategy (397-399)
4. The objective will specify an observable behavior (behavioral objectives 399-400)
5. It will specify the conditions under which the behavior is to occur (399-400)
6. It will specify how well the behavior must be performed (399-400)
7. Developing objectives (student-oriented teaching strategy 399)
8. Selecting activities (402)
9. Creating the learning environment (403)
10. Executing the plans (404)
11. Evaluating the results (405)
12. The student must find it worthwhile (selecting activities 402)
13. It must produce the desired behavior (402)
14. It must be within the student's capabilities (402)
15. Open exchange of ideas (positive psychological environment 403)
16. Free from fear of mistakes (403-404)
17. Positive reinforcement (404)
18. Simple to complex (sequence of activities 401)
19. Known to unknown (401)
20. Whole to part (401)

413

(From part 388)

```
A V E L G U I T A R A G K S
S I D P S M H U U U L G C P
N O R G A N A B K E N L O I
K L B R X D R A U S O A L N
V I O L O N C E L L O S B E
I N B T P T S R E L S S D T
O S O E H R M Y L E S H O M
L I E N O U K L E B A A O A
Y N Z A N M A U N S B R W N
F L U T E P Z O O N E M C D
L C O S V E O J N A B O Y O
A L Q A U T O H A R P N M L
U A X C H E L U T E R I B I
T R O M B O N E J D E C A N
P I A N O O T L A R C A L T
I N E N O H P A S U O S S E
C E L E O B O R E M R A S N
C T I S I T A R R A D I O O
O I T E N R O C N O E B T R
L O I V S S A B A R R I L T
O N A R P O S E P I P G A B
```

414

Answers to Just for Fun

(From part 107)

```
P R E S T O  T A E B D I H X A
A L E N T O E K F W C I A O E
L A N D A N T E T R A P R E U
L R A P O U R Y D O L E M N G
E G P I A N O S F Z F D O P U
G O N T C A F O R M I A N R F
R O G C C L E F D O N L Y C V
O R C H E S R E S T E S O L O
C L L O N G O R H Y T H M O P
S Y A N T I N M E T E R D S M
H R I T A R D A L S I G N E E
A F P C O U N T E R P O I N T
R A L L E N T A N D O G O O M
P T O N O P U S N R O H C T I
T A L F R O N D O M I N A N T
```

(From part 202)

Message 1: Meet me by the old oak at midnight sharp for the microfilm—George

Message 2: A cab will be ready to get you beneath Oldtown Bridge —Al.

Message 3: Can you read C-clef?

Appendix

415

Major Keys: Signatures, Scales and Chords

416

Ab major   I IV V

Eb major   I IV V

Bb major   I IV V

F major   I IV V

Harmonic Minor Keys: Signatures, Scales and Chords

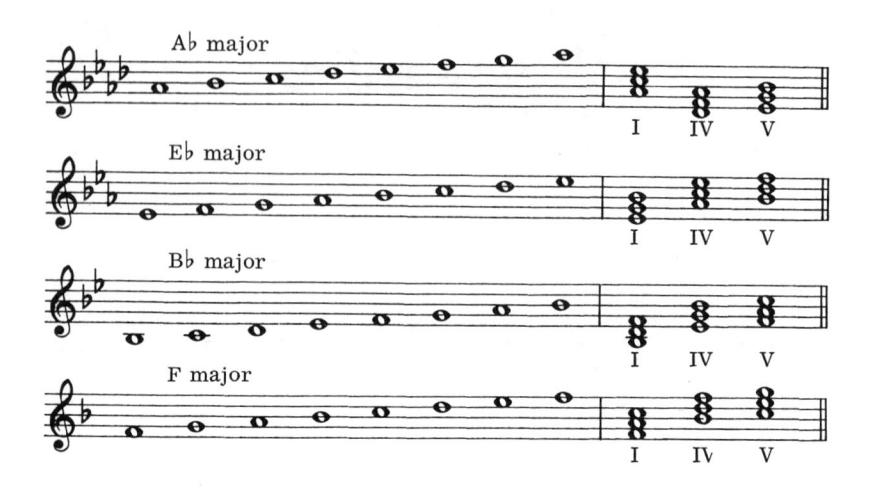

A minor   I IV V

D minor   I IV V

G minor   I IV V

C minor   I IV V

F minor   I IV V

Bb minor   I IV V

Eb minor   I IV V

417

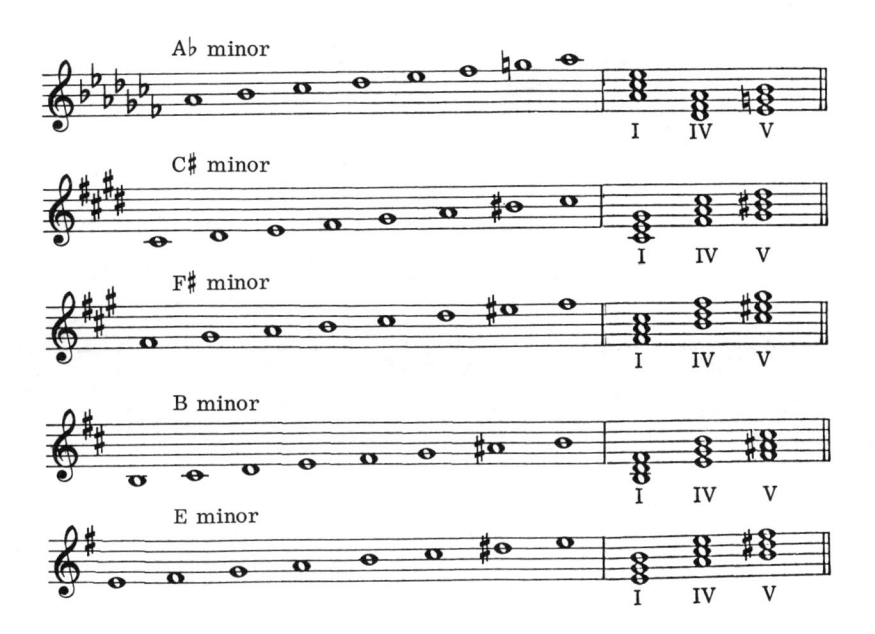

Song Index

A Frog Went A-Courting	292
Alouette	199
America the Beautiful	251
Au Clair de la Lune	354
Billy Boy	200
Bingo	46
Elf in Myself, The	385
Farmer in the Dell	108
Go Tell Aunt Rhody	46
Kobuk Love Song	376
Lili ou Kalani	296
Little Tom Tinker	109
Long, Long Ago	390
Magic of Christmas, The	253
More We Get Together, The	355
Muffin Man	294
O Come, O Come Emmanuel	106
Oh Susanna	340
Old Chairs to Mend	386
Old MacDonald Had a Farm	49
On Top of Old Smokey	353
Polly Wolly Doodle	347
Sleep, Baby, Sleep	392
Swing Low, Sweet Chariot	346
Naughty Boy, The	364
Orchestra Song, The	366
Squirrel, The	363
There was a Woman, Old and Gray	197
This Old Man	45
This Poor Old Slave	295
When Johnny Comes Marching Home	328
Who Has Seen the Wind?	327
Yankee Doodle	107
Yonge's First Catch	378

Index

accent mark, 103
Bach, Orchestra suite
   no. 3, *Air*, 359
bar lines, 7, 81
bass clef
   notes, 126
   sign, 6
binary form, 239, 249

cadence
   authentic, 291
   defined, 258
   half, 340
   mixed, 291
   plagal, 291
chords
   defined, 208
   dominant seventh, 288
   inversions, 246
   names, 275, 277, 282
   primary in key, 277, 285, 313, 316, 320
   substitutes, 282
circle of fifths
   major, 268
   minor, 310
creating music, 289
crescendo, 40

da capo, 36
dal segno, 36
decrescendo, 40
domains of learning, 371
dominant chord, 250, 264
dominant seventh chord, 276
dotted notes, 67
dynamic markings, 39

eighth note, 19
eighth rest, 28

elements, musical, 382
environment for learning, 403
fine, 36
flat, 139
form
   binary, 343, 351, 353, 358
   free, 343, 355
   rondo, 387
   ternary, 343, 351, 353, 358
   theme and variation, 387

great staff, 6

half note, 19
half rest, 28
half steps, 173, 176
harmony
   defined, 208
Haydn, Symphony no. 94, III, 361

instrumental music, 380, 381
interval
   augmented, 225
   defined, 213
   diminshed , 225
   harmonic, 213
   inversions, 234, 235
   major, 225, 227
   minor, 225, 227
   perfect, 225
   sizes, 219

Just for Fun
   fun songs, 295
   Korekteng Badd Speling, 329
   Musical Alphabet Soup, 388

Picturewords, 409
Secret Code, 200
Symbol Addition, 46
Word Square, 106

key
   definition, 258
   relative, 303, 305
   signatures, 192, 269
   tone, 258
keyboard
   black key names, 161
   white key names, 150

learning, theory of, 395
lecture method, 397-399
ledger lines, 116, 139
lesson plan outline, 406

measure, 7
meter signatures, 79, 81
motivation, 396
motive, 336
musical behaviors, primary, 370

natural, 139
notation, devised, 387

objectives
   behavioral, 399
   for elementary music, 373
   scope, 400
   sequence, 401
octave, 145, 166

period, 336
phrase
   antecedent, 340
   consequent, 340
   defined, 336
pickup notes, 99, 100
pitch, musical, 34
primary chords, 263, 275

quarter note, 19
quarter rest, 28

repeat sign, 30
RULEG system, 407

scales
   harmonic minor, 312, 320

   major, 180, 258
   natural minor, 303, 304, 306
   relative, 303, 305
scale tones
   names, 275
   numbers, 261, 263
   tendencies, 263
sequence
   in music, 336
   of objectives, 401
sharp, 139
singing
   evaluation of, 405
   problems with, 380
sixteenth note, 19
sixteenth rest, 28
slur, 103
SOL-FA system, 267, 325
staccato, 103
staff, 6

teaching strategies
   student-oriented, 399
   teacher-oriented, 397
tenuto mark, 103
ternary form, 343, 354
thirds, quality, 227
thought processes, 371
tied notes, 74
time values, 59
tonality, 258
tonic chord, 263, 275
tonic SOL-FA system, 254, 325
treble clef
   notes, 116
   sign, 6
triads
   inversions, 246
   quality, 239

values, formation of, 371, 374

whole note, 19
whole rest, 28
whole steps, 173, 176

OUR LADY BUILDS A STATUE

by

LEROY LEE